D1532809

The Hollywood Cookbook

Cooking for Causes

The Hollywood Cookbook

Cooking for Causes

Jackie Zabel and Morgan Most

The Hollywood Cookbook
ISBN 10: 1-59637-083-1
ISBN 13: 978-1-59637-083-8

Copyright © 2006 Good Looking Cooking

All rights reserved. No part of this book may be used or reproduced in any manner whatsoever
without the prior written permission of the publisher.

Produced by Silverback Books, Inc.
Recipe Testing: Kitchen Academy
Project Editor: Sarah Arak
Food Editor: Rebecca Friend
Design & Layout: Amy Inouye, Future Studio
Photography: Mathew Imaging

*For our loving husbands, Bryce and Don,
and our wonderful, amazing children:
Jonathan, Lauren, Jared, Mackenzie and Madison.*

Contents

Foreword

The menus and unique recipes shared on these pages showcase the great taste and thoughtfulness of an innovative group of people. Grand performances—just like great cooking—require the ongoing search for inspiration. When this type of creativity mixes with the love of good food, you are guaranteed an experience rich with flavor, quality and beauty.

Food is a catalyst for love. Friends invite you to dinner not just for the food, but, for the company and conversation. Grandchildren are brought into the kitchen not just to "help," but also to spend time and share family traditions. And, when that special someone learns how to sear proscuitto-wrapped figs perfectly—just because it's your favorite—you know, this is love.

The Hollywood Cookbook is a truly mouthwatering collection of recipes from both today's most creative talents and world-renowned chefs. Paging through the book is a treat for the imagination. It makes me want to cook with all of the contributing chefs and celebrities! But, it is their motivation for sharing treasured favorites that is perhaps even more powerful: it's about love. Once again, food is the messenger. The wonderful charities that benefit from this book are served dishes that speak from the heart.

At some point, all the contributors—chef and celebrity alike—discovered the artful side of food. As is the way with passionate and creative personalities, they pursue and explore with all their senses. They become frequent visitors of farmers markets, delighting in the organic treasures and herbs. They know how to properly season a pan. They just have to talk about the genius chef at the little place down the street. And, they learn that cooking is a craft that takes a lifetime. Sharing these tastes with others is, in reality, a form of creative expression that serves "art" to people.

Food also is an articulation of culture and individuality. Whether it is a hearty pasta dish or a delicately plated dessert, food preferences reveal so much about our personality, childhood, cooking and entertaining style. Essentially, with this cookbook, you gain a glimpse into the person behind the recipe.

After spending some time in the kitchen with *The Hollywood Cookbook*, you'll find the recipes inspiring and approachable; techniques that home cooks can master. Passionate "foodies"—just like the contributing chefs and celebrities—will enjoy preparing and sharing these dishes. And, just like the contributors, your dishes will look picture-perfect and earn a five-star rating for great taste!

I applaud everyone who made delicious contributions to *The Hollywood Cookbook*. They fill our plates with love for so many worthy causes. From my kitchen to yours, let's all scream: "Hooray for Hollywood"!

CHEF JAMIE GWEN

A Los Angeles based television and radio personality, Chef Jamie Gwen graduated from the prestigious Culinary Institute of America in New York, then continued to pursue her career under the tutelage of many world-renowned chefs. Her live radio show can be heard weekly on Talk Radio 790 KABC and will soon be syndicated nationwide. Jamie also has a long standing association with the Home Shopping Network. Jamie supports multiple charities and loves to volunteer her culinary talents to Girl's Inc. of Orange County, inspiring girls to be smart, strong and bold! Jamie has authored three cookbooks of her own, the latest called *Good Food for Good Times*.

Introduction

Home and Hollywood. Without ever knowing that we would someday embark on this project, we were living in both these worlds. We met when our daughters were in kindergarten twelve years ago and unexpectedly, saw each other again at a Hollywood reception the same night. As moms and creative artists in the entertainment industry, we found ourselves trying to make the most of both of these worlds. Along the way, we became great friends.

And as friends will do, we often found ourselves floating some big ideas. This one stuck. We had both observed the outpouring of love and respect that fans have for celebrities and we talked about how great it would be to harness that positive energy to help people who could use a little of it in their own lives. The idea of this cookbook was born.

Implementation was a new challenge. We were trying to put together a model that really hadn't been done before. Instead of the book benefiting one charity, as many of these cookbooks have done in the past, we wanted to benefit lots of charities. Instead of a single recipe, we wanted to have the opportunity to share an entire meal from each celebrity taking part. We also wanted to highlight the different charities that these talented actors and actresses take time out of their busy schedules to support. And we wanted to know and appreciate why.

As we've gotten to know the different charities, it's now easy to see the attraction. From disease fighting, to children's causes, to environmental concerns, to entertaining the sick, and providing camps for the less fortunate, these are all amazing non-profits. The Art of Elysium brings people art programs to encourage healing. St. Jude Children's Research Hospital never turns a child away. The TreePeople organization inspires people to take care of the environment. Michael J. Fox's Parkinson's Foundation hopes to find a cure for a cruel disease. The Boys and Girls Clubs of America give kids a place to hang out and a sense of community. And that's just a few of the charities named in this cookbook—from which a generous portion of the proceeds will be distributed to each of them by the Entertainment Industry Foundation.

We have discovered many things along the way. Some things were easier than expected, a few were harder. What was easy was finding good-hearted celebrities. Contrary to what the tabloids would have us believe, these people are in the public eye most often because they are great role models. We are very proud to follow their lead in this book, not just in their philanthropic choices, but also on their culinary adventures. And to add further culinary impact, we elicited the aid of some of our country's most accomplished chefs. Wolfgang Puck, Mario Batali, Rocco Dispirito, Joachim Splichal, Michael Cimarusti, and Nick Stellino were each kind enough to provide one of their favorite recipes.

Someone else along the way told us that food brings people together. It's true. Being able to gather and enjoy favorite recipes does help us remember to celebrate the good life we all enjoy. We truly hope that feeling of celebration comes out in this cookbook. We'd love nothing more than for your family and friends to enjoy a meal from the book in the same spirit of *joie de vivre* in which the celebrities offered it. We were so delighted when the chefs at Kitchen Academy confirmed what we suspected: that we actually had a book that also works from a "foodie" point of view.

Many, many people made the cookbook possible in ways large and small. This was not a solo journey, by any means. Contributions came from our generous sponsors, from student chefs, from talented photographers and food stylists, from our great publishing team, from our diligent legal staff, our hard-working accounting department, and our innovative marketing folks. And, of course, there's the understanding and bolstering we received from family and friends. We are indebted to all of them for indulging us this grand idea, and for all of the take out they ate while we were chasing our culinary dreams.

We've always approached everyone involved with the notion that this project would be a win-win situation. Now that it's all come together, we realize we have built this very special community within a community—one with such good feelings. And we are hoping the same for you, the reader. We wish you a lot of great food enjoyed with the accompanying good karma of helping a lot of can-do charities that are trying to change the world for the better. *Bon appetit!*

JACKIE ZABEL
MORGAN MOST

Thora Birch

Thora Birch, who was named for the Norse God Thor, has been acting since early childhood. In her teens she had a major role in the critically acclaimed feature *American Beauty,* which went on to earn five Oscar nominations. She has also had roles in other features such as *Money Trouble, Ghost World,* and *Hocus Pocus.* In 2003, she was Emmy nominated as Outstanding Lead Actress in a Miniseries or a Movie for her lead role in a Lifetime movie called *Homeless to Harvard: The Liz Murray Story.*

Thora Birch   13

ELIZABETH GLASER PEDIATRIC AIDS FOUNDATION

In 1981, Elizabeth Glaser was infected with the AIDS virus through a blood transfusion. Elizabeth and her husband Paul Glaser later learned that Elizabeth had unknowingly passed the virus on to their daughter Ariel and subsequently to their son Jake. At the time, it was not yet widely known that HIV/AIDS impacted children and few understood how HIV affected children differently than adults, leaving children at a serious disadvantage for HIV/AIDS treatment. After Ariel lost her battle against AIDS in 1988, Elizabeth and her two best friends, Susan DeLaurentis and Susie Zeegen, created a foundation with a simple but critical mission: to bring hope to children with AIDS. What began as three moms at a kitchen table more than 17 years ago is now a truly global organization with more than 800 sites in 18 countries dedicated to creating a future of hope for children and families worldwide by eradicating pediatric HIV/AIDS. The Foundation has three main avenues for fighting pediatric AIDS: funding critical research, implementing global health initiatives, and advocating for children's health. Whether the Foundation is working to attract top researchers to the field of pediatric AIDS, creating programs that provide a full continuum of care in developing countries, or working to influence legislators, the programs offer hope for all children afflicted with HIV.

"I chose the Elizabeth Glaser Pediatric AIDS Foundation because it is my favorite children's charity. There are many problems on this earth, and many organizations that address them; however, to me there is nothing more unfair than a life that is scarred from its inception. Children born with HIV should not be strapped with the complications that arise from AIDS, and I believe that it is the responsibility of the more fortunate to reach out to the less fortunate and try to rectify the balance."

—*Thora Birch*

When I began my approach to creating a menu, my main goal was to create a tasty and eclectic, yet coordinated, meal. Only after I had the basic outline of what I wanted to prepare did I start to think about what situation the menu would best suit. In my mind, this meal is for three couples (obviously not on diets!) who want to enjoy themselves to the fullest in an intimate setting. The meal should follow cocktail hour (I'm sure some of the drinks in this book would go perfect with it). With the exception of maybe the cheese sauce (which really only takes about 5 to10 minutes to prepare), everything could be done in advance so that even the host can enjoy his or her own party.

MENU

A Toast to Autumn—
A Great Night with Friends

BLACK BEAN AND SUN-DRIED TOMATO SALAD

SAUTÉED BROCCOLI AND SHIITAKE MUSHROOMS

THREE-CHEESE FETTUCCINE

BERRY AND WHITE CHOCOLATE PUDDING CUPS

© 2006 Thora Birch. Used with permission.

BLACK BEAN AND SUN-DRIED TOMATO SALAD

Serves 6

Ingredients

★ ⅓ cup extra virgin olive oil
★ ½ cup diced sun-dried tomatoes
★ 1½ cups canned black beans, rinsed
★ Kosher salt and freshly ground black pepper
★ 3 cups chopped romaine lettuce
★ 1 cup frozen peas, rinsed and thawed

Directions

1. In a bowl, combine olive oil, sun-dried tomatoes, and beans and season with salt and pepper. Cover and allow to marinate, refrigerated, at least 4 hours and preferably overnight.

2. In a salad bowl, toss lettuce and peas with the dressing.

SAUTÉED BROCCOLI AND SHIITAKE MUSHROOMS

Serves 6

Ingredients

★ 3 cups broccoli florets
★ 2 cups sliced shiitake mushrooms
★ ¼ cup chopped fresh chives
★ 2 teaspoons extra virgin olive oil
★ 1 teaspoon kosher salt

Directions

1. Steam broccoli, mushrooms, and chives (yes, the chives) in a pot until broccoli is tender, about 5 minutes.

2. Heat a sauté pan over medium heat; add oil, vegetables, and salt; and stir. Serve hot.

THREE-CHEESE FETTUCCINE

Serves 6

Ingredients

★ 1 pound fettuccine noodles
(if you can find black-pepper noodles,
go for it!)

★ 4 ounces gorgonzola cheese, crumbled

★ ½ cup grated parmesan cheese

★ ⅔ cup ricotta cheese

★ ¾ cup heavy cream

★ Kosher salt and freshly ground
black pepper

Directions

1. In a large pot of salted water, cook pasta
according to package instructions.

2. While the pasta is cooking, gently heat the
cheese and cream in a saucepan over medium
heat, stirring until smooth, about 3 minutes.
Be careful not to overheat. Season with salt and
pepper.

3. Drain noodles and return to pot. Pour in sauce
and toss well. Serve hot.

BERRY AND WHITE CHOCOLATE PUDDING CUPS

Serves 6

Ingredients

★ 2 (12 ounce) packages Silken Lite® extra firm tofu

★ 1 cup fresh raspberries

★ 1 tablespoon vanilla extract

★ ⅓ cup soy milk

★ 1 (12 ounce) package Hershey's® Premier White Chips

★ 3 tablespoons Equal®

★ 1 package (6 count) mini-graham cracker crusts

Directions

1. In a food processor, mix together tofu, berries, vanilla, soy milk, and Equal in a blender or food processor until smooth. Add the white chips and pulse for 10 seconds. Divide equally into mini-crusts and refrigerate. Serve chilled.

Thora Birch

Michael Chiklis

Emmy-winning actor Michael Chiklis is best known for his role as rogue cop "Vic Mackey," on the television series *The Shield*. But he hasn't limited his acting to the small screen, recently playing "The Thing/Ben Grimm" in the big budget feature film, *The Fantastic Four*. Michael was educated at Boston University's School for the Arts. He is married to Michelle Chiklis and they have two lovely daughters, Autumn and Odessa.

The Children's Lifesaving Foundation is dedicated to improving and enriching the lives of Los Angeles and Ventura Counties' at-risk and homeless youth and their families by financially helping them move out of a shelter into a home and by creating positive opportunities through educational, creative, recreational, and environmental camps. These programs and camps are offered free of charge to at-risk and homeless youth from the ages of infancy through seventeen. Today, the foundation has served well over 27,500 children, and additionally, several hundred parents and families.

"My wife and I recognized how blessed we were as children to have memories such as the one this meal brings up. The opportunity to create these types of memories for children who are less fortunate than we are is a blessing. The Children's Lifesaving Foundation is responsible for creating many such opportunities and life changing experiences. What in the world could be better than that?"
—*Michael Chiklis*

I've always loved this particular meal because it evokes one of my fondest childhood memories. Every Sunday, my brother and I would go out and play in the neighborhood with our friends. While we were out without a care in the world, my parents were engaged in this traditional labor of love. But it wasn't just my family; it was every family in the neighborhood. As a result, the entire neighborhood would take on this delightful aroma. It was something about comfort—about feeling part of a community and family.

MENU

A Walk on the Greek Side

AVGOLEMONO SOUP

SPANAKOPITA

LEG OF LAMB WITH ROASTED POTATOES

BAKLAVA

© 2006 Michael Chiklis. Used with permission.

AVGOLEMONO SOUP

Ingredients

★ 2 quarts chicken broth, cooked
  (boil a chicken and use the broth,
  or use your favorite chicken soup broth)
★ 3 eggs separated (at room temperature)
★ ½ cup rice, cooked
★ Juice of 1½ lemons
★ Salt to taste
★ Flat-leaf Italian parsley

Directions

1. In a bowl, beat egg whites until stiff.
   Add one egg yolk. Continuously beat the egg mixture
   and slowly add the lemon juice. Add rice and salt to
   taste. Continue beating, slowly add the chicken broth,
   one ladle at a time. Serve hot. Garnish with parsley.

SPANAKOPITA

Serves 12

Ingredients

★ 3 (10-ounce) bags prewashed baby spinach

★ 8 eggs, or substitute 1½ pints egg whites, whisked together

★ 1 Maui onion, grated, or substitute other large sweet white onion

★ Fresh ground black pepper

★ 1 box frozen filo dough, thawed overnight in refrigerator

★ 1 cup (2 sticks) unsalted butter, clarified

★ 1½ pounds feta cheese, crumbled

Directions

1. Preheat oven to 350°F.

2. Place spinach in a large mixing bowl. Add eggs and onion, and season with pepper.

3. Grease a 12 × 17 inch baking pan with clarified butter. Lay a sheet of filo dough in the bottom of the pan, lightly brush with butter, then repeat 7 more times. Butter the top layer, then add a ½-inch-thick layer of spinach mixture. Sprinkle with some feta cheese. Top with three more sheets of filo, brushing each with butter before laying the next sheet in. Cover with another layer of spinach mixture and top with more feta cheese. Repeat process until filling ingredients run out and layers reach the top of the pan. Finish with 8 more sheets of filo, lightly buttering each sheet. The dough will be stacked ½ inch above the edge of the pan.

4. Place in the oven and cook, uncovered, for 45 to 60 minutes. Top layer should turn golden brown. Remove from oven and cool for 30 minutes before slicing.

LEG OF LAMB
WITH ROASTED POTATOES

Serves 4-6

Ingredients

★ 1 leg of lamb, about 5-7 pounds (ideally a leg of Spring lamb)
★ 4 tablespoons extra virgin olive oil
★ 4 cloves of garlic, sliced
★ Rind of 1 fresh lemon
★ Juice of 4 lemons
★ 8 potatoes, unpeeled, sliced into wedges
★ 8 tablespoons (1 stick) butter, sliced into pats
★ 2 sprigs fresh oregano, chopped
★ 2 sprigs fresh parsley, chopped
★ Kosher salt and freshly ground black pepper
★ 1 whole onion, grated
★ ¼ cup brown sugar
★ ½ cup good quality red wine

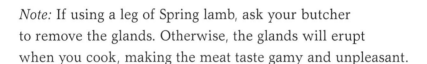

Note: If using a leg of Spring lamb, ask your butcher
to remove the glands. Otherwise, the glands will erupt
when you cook, making the meat taste gamy and unpleasant.

Directions

1. Preheat oven to 350°F.

2. Rub lamb with olive oil. Using a sharp knife, poke 1-inch-deep holes
   into flesh and fill with slices of garlic.

3. Place lamb in a roasting pan greased with olive oil, and surround with
   potatoes and lemon rind. Pour in ½ cup water and the lemon juice.
   Add butter pats evenly over the lamb and potatoes. Add salt, pepper,
   oregano, parsley, and grated onion. Sprinkle with brown sugar and
   cover with foil.

4. Cook for 3 hours. Baste with ½ cup red wine and pan juices. Return
   to oven, and baste every thirty minutes. After 4 hours, remove cover
   and let the meat brown; cook for 1 additional hour. Total cooking time
   is 5 hours. Remove from oven: let meat rest, covered in foil, for
   15 minutes. Serve sliced with pan juices.

BAKLAVA

Serves 12

Ingredients

- ★ 3 cups water
- ★ 3 cups sugar
- ★ 1 tablespoon lemon juice
- ★ 1 box frozen filo dough, thawed overnight in refrigerator
- ★ 4 cups chopped walnuts.
- ★ ½ cup sugar
- ★ 1 tablespoon ground cinnamon
- ★ 1 cup (2 sticks) unsalted butter, clarified

Directions

1. In a small pot, boil water, sugar, and lemon juice for fifteen minutes, stirring frequently, reducing to a syrup. Set aside and let cool.

2. Mix the walnuts, sugar, and cinnamon together.

3. Grease a 12 × 17 inch baking pan with clarified butter. Lay in a sheet of filo dough, lightly brush with butter, then repeat 7 more times. Butter the top layer, then add half of the walnut mixture. Top with three more sheets of filo, brushing each with butter before laying in the next sheet. Cover with the other half of the walnut mixture. Finish with 8 more sheets of filo, lightly buttering each sheet. Place in refrigerator until the butter is hardened.

4. Preheat oven to 350°F.

5. Slice into diamonds, cutting lengthwise and then diagonally across, slicing completely through to the bottom. Bake for 35 minutes, or until golden brown. Remove from the oven and cover with syrup. Allow to cool before serving.

Mario Batali

With a restaurant empire, several cookbooks, a line of food products, and appearances on television and in print too numerous to mention, it is hard to discuss current culinary trends in America without citing the name of Mario Batali. Raised in Seattle, Mario graduated from college and began to study at Le Cordon Bleu in London but quickly withdrew because of a lack of interest. He next apprenticed with the great Chef Marco Pierre White and then spent three years of intense culinary training in the small northern Italian village of Borgo Capanne. Mario returned to the United States and, in 1998, opened Babbo Ristorante e Enoteca in New York City to much critical acclaim. The James Beard Foundation named Babbo "Best New Restaurant of 1998," and Mario continued his success with the opening of several more New York City restaurants. He is a featured chef on the Food Network show, *Iron Chef America.*

GOAT CHEESE TORTELLONI
WITH DRIED ORANGE AND FENNEL POLLEN

Makes 60 Tortelloni

Serves 6

The trick to this dish is making sure that the filling is quite moist. Once cooked and plated, the soft filling should ooze out of the cut tortelloni like ripened Brie that has spent hours on the counter. Fennel pollen was very difficult to find when I first tasted it at Macelleria Cecchini in Panzano, but now it seems ubiquitous.

Ingredients

★ 2 cups fresh goat cheese, preferably Coach Farm® brand

★ 1 cup milk

★ 1 tablespoon finely chopped parsley

★ 10 sage leaves, finely chopped

★ 1 teaspoon finely chopped fresh rosemary

★ 1 tablespoon finely chopped fresh thyme

★ ½ teaspoon freshly grated nutmeg

★ ½ cup freshly grated Parmigiano-Reggiano

★ Kosher salt and freshly ground black pepper

★ 1½ recipes basic pasta dough, prepared

★ ½ cup (1 stick) unsalted butter

★ 12 to 14 clean, beautiful fennel fronds

★ 2 teaspoons narrow orange zest strips, dried in a 200°F oven for 30 minutes

★ 1 tablespoon fennel pollen or ground fennel seeds

Directions

1. In a large bowl, mash the goat cheese with the milk until soft. Add the herbs, nutmeg, ¼ cup of the Parmigiano, salt, and pepper and stir well. Cover the mixture and refrigerate until firm, about 30 minutes.

2. Using a pasta machine, roll out the pasta to the thinnest setting and then cut the sheets into 4 inch squares. Place 1 tablespoon of the goat cheese filling in the center of each square. Fold two opposite corners together to form a triangle and press the edges together firmly to seal. Bring the long points of the triangle together in a ring and join with firm finger pressure. Continue filling and shaping the tortelloni until all the pasta and fillings are used. At this point you may freeze the tortelloni on cookie sheets between layers of waxed paper. Transfer to plastic bags and store in the freezer for up to a week.

3. Bring 6 quarts of water to a boil and add 2 tablespoons of salt. Drop the tortelloni into the boiling water and cook until tender, 3 to 5 minutes. Carefully drain the tortelloni, reserving about 1 cup of the pasta water.

4. Meanwhile, in a sauté pan, heat the butter and one-fourth of the pasta water together, whisking to form an emulsified sauce. Add the cooked tortelloni, fennel fronds, and orange zest to the pan to heat gently and coat with the sauce, about 1 minute. Divide among 6 warmed plates, topping the tortelloni with fennel fronds and orange zest. Finish with a sprinkling of fennel pollen and the remaining ¼ cup of Parmigiano-Reggiano and serve immediately.

BASIC PASTA DOUGH

Ingredients

* ★ 3½ to 4 cups all-purpose flour
* ★ 4 extra-large eggs
* ★ ½ teaspoon extra virgin olive oil

Directions

1. Mound 3½ cups of the flour in the center of a large wooden cutting board. Make a well in the middle of the flour and add the eggs and the olive oil. Using a fork, beat together the eggs and oil and begin to incorporate the flour, starting with the inner rim of the well.

2. As you expand the well, keep pushing the flour up from the base of the mound to retain the well shape. The dough will come together when half of the flour is incorporated.

3. Start kneading the dough with both hands, using the palms of your hands. Once you have a cohesive mass, remove the dough from the board and scrape up and discard any leftover bits. Lightly reflour the board and continue kneading for 6 more minutes. The dough should be elastic and a little sticky. Wrap the dough in plastic and allow to rest for 30 minutes at room temperature.

4. Roll the pasta out on a pasta rolling machine to the desired thickness.

Eric Close

Eric Close has become a fixture on network television. His credits include his portrayals of "Martin Fitzgerald" on *Without a Trace*, "Vin Tanner" on the *Magnificent Seven,* and "John Loengard" on *Dark Skies.* Eric grew up in San Diego, and went on to get a bachelor's degree in communications from the University of Southern California. Eric married Keri in 1995 and they have two daughters, Katie and Ella.

I n 1995, Crystal Peaks Youth Ranch was created in an effort to
foster hope and an empowered future for youth. It's a place where
children of all ages can experience the healing embrace and life
changing bond with horses. When started in 1995, Crystal Peaks was
the only organization of its kind in the United States. What made it so
very unique back then was that nearly all of the 25 horses that lived on
the ranch were rescued from violent abuse or life-threatening neglect.
Today, thanks to the leadership of Crystal Peaks, 23 additional ranches
have been formed across the United States and Canada. Leaders from
each of these facilities have been to the ranch and are using Crystal
Peaks programming to reach the youth of their respective communities.
This programming, while simple in nature, pairs one horse, one child,
and one leader, 100 percent of the time. Through hands-on experience,
the organization teaches kids the values of life, family, and trust.
Children, horses, and families find hope within the healing circle of
unconditional love. The group's "one on one" learning environment is
dedicated to restoring the heart, soul, mind, and strength of our kids.

"A few years ago, while working on the series *McKenna* in Bend, Oregon, I met Kim and Troy Meeder. They are two of the most incredible people I have ever known. Just around the time we met, Kim and Troy had cashed in their life savings in order to start Crystal Peaks Youth Ranch. The Ranch is now home to horses that were rescued from starvation, abuse, or severe neglect. For more than ten years, this unique nonprofit organization has been pairing hurting and disadvantaged children with the horses. More than 30,000 children have found hope and healing through this program, free of cost to anyone. Crystal Peaks Youth Ranch works closely with school districts, private counselors, and the Juvenile Justice Department to name a few. The results of this program have been miraculous. This is why Keri and I chose Crystal Peaks Youth Ranch as our charity."

—*Eric Close*

We love to have family and friends over as much as possible. With my crazy and unpredictable schedule, we like to have a few simple recipes on hand that can be made on short notice. The turkey burgers are moist and flavorful and a great alternative to beef. The salad is light and refreshing. The corn on the cob is my mom's secret Hungarian recipe—the corn is so moist and sweet prepared in this manner. The apple crisp is Keri's mom's super-easy recipe. This party menu can be served all year round, but summertime is our favorite. So call your closest buddies, whip up some burgers, and enjoy!

MENU

Without a Trace of Leftovers— Our Favorite Backyard BBQ

CREAM CHEESE SALSA DIP

SALAD WITH MANDARIN ORANGES
AND SLIVERED ALMONDS

SPECIAL CORN ON THE COB

KERI'S FAMOUS MUSHROOM TURKEY BURGERS

NANA'S APPLE CRISP

CREAM CHEESE SALSA DIP

Serves 4 to 6

Ingredients

★ 1 (8 ounce) tub of cream cheese

★ 1½ cups of your favorite salsa

★ 1 bag tortilla chips, preferably blue corn

Directions

1. Place cream cheese in medium-sized bowl and warm, briefly (about 30 seconds), in a microwave. Remove from microwave and top with salsa. Serve with tortilla chips.

SALAD WITH MANDARIN ORANGES AND SLIVERED ALMONDS

Serves 6

Ingredients

★ ¼ cup olive oil
★ 2 tablespoons white wine vinegar
★ 2 tablespoons plus ¼ cup sugar
★ 1½ tablespoons chopped fresh parsley
★ Few dashes Tabasco sauce
★ Pinch freshly ground black pepper
★ 2½ cups slivered almonds
★ 3 romaine hearts, roughly chopped
★ 1 cup chopped scallions
★ 1 15-ounce can mandarin oranges

Directions

1. Combine oil, vinegar, 2 tablespoons sugar, parsley, hot sauce, and black pepper in an airtight container and shake well until combined and sugar is dissolved. Set aside.

2. Place almonds and ¼ cup sugar in a sauté pan over medium-low heat. Stir until sugar has melted and coated almonds. Remove from pan and place on plate to cool.

3. Toss lettuce and scallions together in bowl. Top with almonds and mandarin oranges. Toss with dressing and serve.

Note: Turn this salad into a meal by adding grilled shrimp.

SPECIAL CORN ON THE COB

Serves 8

Ingredients

★ 8 ears fresh corn, shucked and rinsed

★ 1 cup whole milk

★ ½ cup butter plus additional for serving

★ Paprika

Directions

1. Place corn ears in large pot and just
   cover with water. Add milk and butter
   to water, cover and bring to a boil.
   Reduce heat and simmer for 3 minutes.
   Remove from heat and let sit for
   5 minutes. Drain and discard liquid.
   Sprinkle with paprika and serve hot
   with butter.

Eric Close   43

KERI'S FAMOUS MUSHROOM TURKEY BURGERS

Serves 6

Ingredients

★ 1½ pounds ground turkey meat
★ 1 cup mushrooms, cleaned
★ 1 cup Italian-style bread crumbs
★ 2 cloves garlic
★ 2 teaspoons seasoned salt
★ Freshly ground black pepper
★ 1 egg white
★ Nonstick spray
★ 6 burger buns

Directions

1. Place mushrooms into the bowl of a food processor and pulse for 30 seconds. Add bread crumbs, garlic, salt, and pepper and blend thoroughly.

2. Place ground turkey in large bowl: add mushroom mixture and egg white. Mix well and form into 6 patties.

3. Spray a heated grill or grill pan with nonstick spray and cook, turning once, for 6 to 7 minutes per side, until juices run clear when poked in the center.

4. Serve on your favorite bun with a selection of condiments, such as sliced avocado, chopped onion, sliced cheese, shredded lettuce, and ketchup and mustard.

NANA'S APPLE CRISP

Serves 8

Ingredients

★ 8 Granny Smith apples, peeled, cored, and sliced thinly

★ ½ cup butter, divided into pats

★ 1 teaspoon plus 1 tablespoon ground cinnamon

★ ½ cup butter, melted

★ 1 cup sugar

★ 1 cup all-purpose flour

★ 1 cup minute oats

Directions

1. Preheat oven to 350°F.

2. Place apples into a 9×13×2 baking dish. Top with ½ cup butter pats and sprinkle with 1 teaspoon cinnamon.

3. In a mixing bowl, combine melted butter, sugar, flour, oats, and 1 tablespoon cinnamon and stir until crumbly. Spread topping evenly over apples.

4. Bake for 45 minutes to 1 hour, until lightly browned and crispy. Serve warm with vanilla ice cream.

Mark Dacascos

Mark Dacascos is not only a skilled actor, but also a world-renowned martial artist. On top of all that, Mark also intersects the culinary world as the "Chairman" on Food Network's *Iron Chef America*. Not surprisingly, in view of his diverse interests, Mark maintains an incredibly busy schedule—in the past two years alone, Mark has been cast in five different feature films. Mark is married to actress Julie Condra and they have two sons and a daughter.

Mark Dacascos   47

Reel Angels™

Reel Angels is dedicated to lifting the spirits of hospitalized children through the magic of first-run films. Most children with serious illnesses are hospitalized for months at a time. Even if they make brief visits home, they are often unable to spend a Saturday at the movies or enjoy other simple childhood pleasures because of their weakened immune systems. But just like their healthy friends and siblings, sick children eagerly look forward to each big movie. We all know that waiting even a few months for a DVD release can seem like an eternity for most kids, and for some, time is very precious. Rather than allowing these special kids to feel left out, Reel Angels helps restore some normalcy to their lives. By bringing the films to them while still in theaters, Reel Angels helps them escape their surroundings: the gray walls, the ominous equipment, and tinted windows. Even if just for a couple of hours, the kids get a chance to leave some of their pain behind, spend quality time with their families, and smile at the stories and pictures unfolding before them.

"Reel Angels is the charity we'd like to dedicate our luau recipes to. It's a wonderful organization that brings first-run family movies to children who are unable to leave the hospital. Many of the children who are long term inpatients spend most of their days in monotony and pain, with television being one of their few pleasures. The kids see a trailer of a movie they'd like to see, but they know that they won't be able to go to the theater and therefore won't see the film until it's released on DVD many months later. Reel Angels brings those movies to the children as soon as the film comes out. Showing those inspiring and entertaining movies helps bring some joy and hope to the lives of the little ones who need it most."

—Mark Dacascos

I was born in Hawaii and raised there until I was six, so my taste buds developed an inherent love for "local" food. When I am home, my favorite things to eat are a "plate lunch" (especially after a surf session), anything that has just been pulled out of the beautiful Hawaiian waters, or anything at my favorite restaurant, Alan Wong's. Living on the "mainland" (the continental United States), my family and I keep Hawaii fresh in our hearts via our stomachs. My wife, Julie, is from Texas and knows how to cook! With help from our kids, we start the festive day making my Auntie Gwen's Banana Pancakes for breakfast. Add to them some coconut syrup, and I am instantly transported back to another wonderful time when I'd walk hand in hand with my Grandma to Waikiki Beach, or go fishing on Sunday with my Grandpa at the Marine base in Kaneohe.

Even if you are not from the Islands, using ingredients such as pineapple, macadamia nuts, and coconut can at least bring your palate closer to what is, geographically speaking, the most isolated island chain in the world, as well as the most southern state of our nation (I really get my wife with that one!)—which accounts for our kind of southern hospitality aloha! I hope you find the luau dishes as *ono* (delicious) as I do. *Allez cuisine!*

Aloha Local Boy Luau

AUNTIE GWEN'S BANANA PANCAKES

PINEAPPLE MARTINIS

BRIE AND MACADAMIA NUT DEEP-FRIED WONTONS
WITH PINEAPPLE MARMALADE

GINGER CRUSTED FISH WITH CORN, MUSHROOMS,
AND MISO-SESAME VINAIGRETTE

FINGER LICKIN' HOISIN BABY BACK RIBS

BANANA LUMPIA WITH COCONUT ICE CREAM

AUNTIE GWEN'S BANANA PANCAKES

Serves 4

Ingredients

★ 2 cups flour
★ ½ cup sugar
★ 2 eggs
★ 1½ cups of milk
★ 1 teaspoon vanilla extract
★ 5 apple bananas, or substitute regular bananas, peeled and sliced into ½ inch rounds
★ Vegetable oil
★ Coconut syrup
★ Butter

Directions

1. Mix together flour, sugar, eggs, milk, and vanilla. Stir in banana slices.

2. Heat ½ inch oil in a large frying pan. Pour batter into oil and cook, gently turning over once, taking care not to splatter oil. Cook until golden on both sides.

3. Place on paper towel to drain. Top with butter and coconut syrup. *Ono!!!*

PINEAPPLE MARTINIS

Serves 12

"Now, you will need to start this one a few days ahead. After much taste testing, we have found that three days is about perfect! I suggest that everyone leaves his or her car keys in a bowl to be claimed at the end of the night, *if* the person is safe to drive. These sweet, tasty drinks can creep up on you! They are *very* easy to drink! Before you know it, every one will be doing the Hula!

Note: This recipe is a guideline. We generally triple this recipe in a very large glass container with a spigot at the bottom. It is always empty at the end of the evening!"

Ingredients

★ 1 liter of premium vodka
★ 2 large pineapples, peeled, cored, and cut into small cubes

Directions

1. In a large glass jar, combine the pineapples and vodka and store, refrigerated, for three days. If is isn't sweet enough and still has an alcohol taste, add more pineapple and keep it in the refrigerator 1 additional day. Strain, reserving cubed pineapple for garnish.

2. To serve, pour into martini glasses. Garnish with pineapple cubes on an umbrella pick. *Cheers!*

BRIE AND MACADAMIA NUT DEEP FRIED WONTONS
WITH PINEAPPLE MARMALADE

"Nobody said this was health food, but it is delicious!!"

24 wontons

Ingredients

★ 2 cups chopped fresh or canned pineapple

★ 1 cup sugar

★ Pinch of red hot pepper flakes . . .
to give it a kick!

★ 8 ounces Brie cheese cut into cubes

★ 24 wonton wrappers

★ ½ cup crushed macadamia nuts

★ 2 egg whites, whisked together

★ Oil for frying

Directions

1. In a saucepan, combine pineapple and sugar.
   Bring to a boil over medium heat and cook until it
   thickens like syrup, stirring occasionally, for about
   45 minutes for fresh pineapple and less for canned.
   Set aside.

2. Brush a wonton wrapper with egg white. Put a
   cube of Brie in the middle. Sprinkle with chopped
   macadamia nuts. Press cheese down while gathering
   up the wrapper just above the cheese and seal like
   a little present, fanning out at the top. Repeat with
   remaining wonton ingredients.

3. In a wok or heavy pot, heat the oil to 375°F. Deep
   fry until wonton is golden and cheese is melted in
   the middle, about 2 to 3 minutes. Serve with the
   marmalade.

GINGER CRUSTED FISH
WITH CORN, MUSHROOMS, AND MISO-SESAME VINAIGRETTE

"This dish is our all-time favorite thing to eat on the planet. It is a little work, but once you've done it, you will want to do it over and over! Make the Vinaigrette and Ginger Scallion Oil in advance. That way, on the day of the party, all you have to do is sear the fish and assemble."

Serves 4

Ingredients
Miso-Sesame Vinaigrette:

★ ½ cup rice wine vinegar

★ ¼ cup chicken stock

★ 3 tablespoons white miso paste

★ 3 tablespoons sugar

★ 2 tablespoons chunky peanut butter

★ 2 teaspoons minced ginger

★ 1 teaspoon minced garlic

★ 1 jalapeño chili, seeds removed

★ 2 teaspoons honey mustard

★ 1 cup vegetable oil

★ 2 teaspoons dark sesame oil

Directions

1. In a food processor or blender, combine all ingredients except oils and purée until smooth. With the motor running, slowly add the vegetable oil and then sesame oil until incorporated. Store, refrigerated, until needed.

Ingredients
Ginger Scallion Oil:

★ ¼ cup minced ginger

★ ¼ cup minced scallions, green parts only

★ ¼ cup peanut oil

★ 1/8 teaspoon dark sesame oil

★ Pinch of kosher salt

Directions

1. Place ginger and scallions in a deep bowl. Heat peanut oil until just smoking. Pour hot oil over ginger mixture. Be careful— it moves around in the bowl. Add sesame oil and salt to taste. Store, refrigerated, until needed. (This can also be drizzled over anything you want to grill.)

Ingredients

Fish:

★ ¼ cup peanut oil

★ 4 fish fillets

★ salt and pepper

★ ½ cup Ginger Scallion Oil

★ ½ cup panko (Japanese breadcrumbs)

★ 2 teaspoons butter

★ ½ cup sliced shiitake mushrooms

★ ½ cup fresh corn kernels (canned are fine, drained well)

★ ¼ cup yellow pepper, finely diced

Directions

1. Preheat oven to 375°F.

2. In a sauté pan over high heat, heat peanut oil until extremely hot. Season fish with salt and pepper, and sear fish for 45 seconds on each side or until browned.

3. Place fish into a baking dish and top with Ginger Scallion Oil (chunks and all) and sprinkle panko on top. Bake 6 minutes or until tender and cooked through.

4. Meanwhile, melt butter in sauté pan. Add mushrooms and peppers and cook for 3-4 minutes, then add corn and cook 2 more minutes.

5. To serve, divide vegetables among 4 plates. Pour Miso-Sesame Vinaigrette around vegetables and top with fish. Be prepared to hand out the recipe.

FINGER LICKIN' HOISIN BABY BACK RIBS

"My southern wife feels well represented with these ribs on the table. They have what she calls 'comfort food' quality, but the flavor is pure Hawaiian! We like to have most of the prep work done before the day of the party. These are great because you marinate them a day in advance. All that's left is to grill and bake. We do that early in the afternoon and keep it warm."

Serves 6

Ingredients
- ★ ¾ cup Hoisin sauce
- ★ 1 cup ketchup
- ★ ½ cup honey
- ★ 5 tablespoons soy sauce
- ★ 5 tablespoons dry sherry
- ★ ¼ cup plus 2 teaspoons curry powder
- ★ 2 tablespoons plus 2 teaspoons dark sesame oil
- ★ 2 tablespoons grated orange zest
- ★ 2 tablespoons dry fermented black beans (available at Asian markets)
- ★ 2 tablespoons minced garlic
- ★ 1 tablespoon minced Serrano chilies
- ★ 3 pounds (2 racks) baby back pork ribs
- ★ Kosher salt and freshly ground black pepper

Directions

1. Combine the first eleven ingredients (all but the ribs, salt, and pepper) in a bowl and mix thoroughly.

2. Divide ribs between two baking dishes and brush with half of sauce, reserving the other half of the sauce, covered. Refrigerate ribs overnight.

3 Heat the grill and preheat the oven to 350°F. Remove the ribs from the marinade and season with salt and pepper. Grill for 15 minutes, turning frequently. Transfer ribs to roasting pan, add 1 inch of water and cover with foil. Cook in the oven for 2 hours or until tender (go check the martinis!). Remove from the pan and let cool. Bring the remaining sauce to a simmer. Cut ribs individually and pass with heated sauce.

BANANA LUMPIA
WITH COCONUT ICE CREAM

12 Lumpia

Ingredients

★ 12 egg roll wrappers

★ 6 bananas, peeled and halved

★ 1 cup brown sugar

★ 2 eggs, beaten

★ Optional ingredients: cinnamon, crushed macadamia nuts, chopped lychees, dried cranberries . . . have fun and be creative!

★ Vegetable oil for frying

★ Coconut ice cream

Directions

1. Brush 1 wrapper with egg wash. Place a half banana inside wrapper with 1 tablespoon brown sugar and any optional ingredients as desired. Roll, folding in ends to seal in banana. Repeat with remaining wrappers and filling.

2. In a wok or heavy pot, heat the oil to 375°F. Deep fry lumpia until golden, about 30 to 40 seconds. Drain on paper towels. Cut crosswise and serve with coconut ice cream.

James Denton

Hailing from Nashville, Tennessee, James Denton is well known to viewers of the popular ABC TV show *Desperate Housewives* for his role as "Mike Delfino," the plumber. James has played guest roles on many television dramas as well, including *The Pretender, The Untouchables, JAG, Sliders, Dark Skies,* and *Ally McBeal.* James started his career in Chicago theater before moving to Hollywood. He and his wife Erin O'Brien Denton have two children.

James Denton 59

Cure Autism Now is an organization of parents, clinicians, and scientists dedicated to accelerating research to prevent, treat, and cure autism—for individuals and families today, and for future generations. Founded by parents of children with autism in 1995, the organization has grown from a kitchen-table effort to become a national research, education, and outreach leader. Through funding to date of more than $31 million in research awards and the development and support of the Autism Genetic Resource Exchange (AGRE), Cure Autism Now has become one of the largest private funders of autism research in the country. Cure Autism Now is committed to broadening awareness and understanding of a disorder that now affects an estimated one in every 166 children born in the United States.

"I have chosen as my beneficiary the Cure Autism Now Foundation. I first heard about Cure Autism Now is the fall of 2004, when my wife, Erin, and I received an invitation to a benefit in Los Angeles. Autism has been in the news and, as parents of two young children, my wife and I understand why families affected by autism need help. In fact, not long before, Erin had learned that autism had struck in her family as her brother-in-law's nephew, Aidan, is affected. Although autism is a complex neuro-developmental disorder, its common traits are impairment of communication and social interaction. Children with autism often need special education and a variety of treatments and therapies, and their families make enormous emotional and financial investments in their well-being. My wife and I are proud to advocate on behalf of these families and support Cure Autism Now's mission to find the causes, effective treatments, and a cure for autism."

—*James Denton*

Growing up in Tennessee, I've always loved Southern cooking and I've gotten my wife, Erin, who is from Minnesota, to develop a taste for this downhome-type cuisine as well. I wanted to share these particular recipes because they represent some great examples from a Southern palette. Biscuits and gravy aren't just for Thanksgiving but can be enjoyed all year around. Also, the spinach and strawberry salad isn't necessarily something that sounds good, but trust me, it's a wonderful combination of sweet and sour. Grits are a very basic taste but, when made in this soufflé recipe with cheese, very satisfying. Baked apple is a light dessert but no less tasty, and what's really amazing about it is how good it makes the house smell when cooking.

Southern Comfort Foods

CHEESE GRITS SOUFFLÉ

BISCUITS AND GRAVY

SPINACH AND STRAWBERRY SALAD

STUFFED AND BAKED APPLES

CHEESE GRITS SOUFFLÉ

Serves 6

Ingredients

★ 2 cups water
★ ½ cup quick-cooking grits
★ 2 ounces shredded cheese
  (I recommend horseradish Cheddar)
★ ¼ cup butter
★ 2 eggs
★ ⅓ cup lowfat milk
★ Freshly grated parmesan cheese
★ Pinch paprika (optional)

Directions

1. Preheat oven to 350°F.

2. Place the water in a small saucepan and bring to a boil over medium-high heat. Turn the heat to low and slowly stir or whisk in the grits. Beat with a wire whisk to eliminate any lumps.

3. Turn the heat down to a minimum and cover pan. Cook for 5 to 10 minutes, until water is absorbed and grits are creamy. Remove from heat and scrape into a mixing bowl. Add the butter and cheese and stir until they are combined.

4. In separate bowl, beat together eggs and milk. Combine this with the grits.

5. Pour into an 8 × 8 inch baking dish or 6 ramekins. Top with grated parmesan. Add a dash of paprika if you like. Bake, uncovered, for 45 minutes to an hour in baking dish, or 30 minutes in ramekins, until top is golden brown.

James Denton   63

BISCUITS AND GRAVY

Serves 6

Ingredients
Biscuits:
★ 2 cups self-rising flour
★ ¼ to ½ cup shortening
★ ¼ cup milk

Directions

1. Preheat oven to 425°F.

2. Cut shortening with flour until you get coarse texture. Add milk quickly. Sprinkle flour on flat surface, and knead dough.

3. Roll out to about ¾ of an inch thickness. Cut biscuits with a round cutter. Dip biscuits in flour so they won't stick.

4. Bake for 10 to 15 minutes until golden brown.

Ingredients
Gravy:
★ ½ pound sausage, preferably bulk, crumbled
★ 4 tablespoons all-purpose flour
★ 2½ cups milk
★ Kosher salt and freshly ground black pepper

Directions

1. In a sauté pan over medium heat, cook sausage until brown. Pour off excess grease, leaving about 2 tablespoons, and add the flour 1 tablespoon at a time, until incorporated. Cook until flour starts to brown, then add the milk slowly, stirring constantly. Season with salt and pepper. Continue cooking until gravy thickens.

2. Divide biscuits among plates, and smother with gravy.

SPINACH and STRAWBERRY SALAD

Serves 6

Ingredients

★ ¾ cup vegetable oil

★ 1½ tablespoons Dijon mustard

★ ¼ teaspoon kosher salt

★ 3 tablespoons balsamic vinegar

★ 3 tablespoons plus 1 teaspoon freshly squeezed lemon juice

★ 1½ tablespoons sugar

★ 4½ cups baby spinach, washed and dried

★ 2½ cups strawberries, washed and sliced

★ ⅓ red onion, sliced thin

Directions

1. Combine vegetable oil, mustard, salt, vinegar, lemon juice, and sugar in a bowl and whisk thoroughly.

2. In serving bowl, toss together spinach, strawberries, and red onion. Drizzle with dressing and serve immediately.

STUFFED AND BAKED APPLES

Serves 6

Ingredients

★ ⅔ cup brown sugar

★ 4 tablespoons butter (½ stick), plus extra for pan

★ ¼ cup chopped pecans

★ ¼ cup raisins

★ 6 large apples (ask your grocer for best baking apples)

★ 3 cinnamon sticks, cut in half

Directions

1. Preheat oven to 300°F.

2. In a bowl, cream together the sugar and butter, then add pecans and raisins.

3. Core the apples, leaving apples intact by not coring all the way through to the bottom, removing about 2 tablespoons of flesh from each apple.

4. Fill each apple with ⅙ of the mixture, and place apples into a buttered baking dish. Insert a half cinnamon stick into each apple.

5. Bake for 30 minutes, until apples soften.

Michael Cimarusti

Michael Cimarusti's culinary journey began on the East Coast, where Cimarusti went fishing nearly every weekend. Fascinated by all things related to food and the restaurant world and raised in a family where Italian heritage and traditions ran deep, Cimarusti learned that cooking was more than a hobby. Like many aspiring chefs, Cimarusti attended the Culinary Institute of America in Hyde Park, New York, where he graduated with honors in 1990. With loads of culinary knowledge in his head and a diploma in hand, Cimarusti headed to New York City. Eventually, he began a three-year relationship at Le Cirque working alongside culinary greats. Cimarusti then headed for Hollywood after accepting a position as chef de cuisine at the original Spago. He also worked at the Water Grill before taking his position with his current Los Angeles fine dining restaurant, Providence.

GRILLED SPOT PRAWNS
WITH CRISPY VEGETABLES

"Spot prawns are a true treasure of the Pacific Coast. They are difficult to find, but when you do find them, you will never be disappointed. Simply boiled, they are miraculous. Grilled or roasted, they take on a different flavor altogether. You can substitute head-on shrimp of several varieties, or substitute fresh sardines for the shrimp. I would use the biggest sardines you can find—Japanese Iwashi are the best. I would bone them out and cook them as quickly as possible over high heat on the grill. The vegetables that accompany are meant to mirror and highlight the crisp nature of the prawns. The vegetables should be very lightly dressed, and should hold their shapes when standing off the plate. The herbs will provide little bursts of flavor and will play off the richness of the shrimp."

—*Michael Cimarusti*

GRILLED SPOT PRAWNS
WITH CRISPY VEGETABLES

Serves 8

Ingredients

★ 4 French breakfast radishes, or other radishes, washed well
★ 8 yellow baby carrots
★ 8 orange baby carrots
★ 4 baby turnips
★ 1 small red onion
★ 1 small Japanese cucumber
★ 12 asparagus
★ 1 teaspoon fresh parsley leaves
★ 1 teaspoon fresh chervil leaves
★ 1 teaspoon fresh tarragon leaves
★ Tender yellow celery leaves from one head of celery
★ Juice and zest of one lemon
★ 1 cup extra virgin olive oil
★ 12 Santa Barbara Spot prawns
★ Fleur de sel and white pepper

Directions

1. To begin, peel and trim all of the vegetables. For the carrots, turnips, and the radishes, keep ½ inch of the green stem attached. Peel and trim the asparagus tips so that they are 2 inches long, reserving the stems for some other purpose.

2 Next prepare a large bowl of ice water. Shave the vegetables with a Japanese mandoline as thinly as possible and place in ice water. Add the herbs and the celery leaves to the ice water as well. Let the vegetables sit in the ice water until they take on a crispy texture. Drain the vegetables and dry in a salad spinner. Set the vegetables aside in the refrigerator.

3. Prepare a charcoal or wood fire. Place the live prawns on the grill and cook on each side for 3 minutes. Allow the shells of the prawns to char slightly, as this will heighten their flavor. Remove the prawns from the grill and allow them to rest for a moment.

4. Place the vegetables in a large mixing bowl and season with fleur de sel and freshly ground white pepper. Drizzle with olive oil, lemon juice, and lemon zest, and toss.

5. Divide vegetables among the plates. Split the prawns and lay three halves over the vegetables. Collect any prawn juices and spoon over the prawns. Season the split prawns with fleur de sel and a few turns of white pepper. Drizzle the plates with a splash of olive oil and serve immediately.

Michael Cimarusti

Michael J. Fox

Michael J. Fox came to Hollywood from Canada at the age of eighteen, and began to land some of the most memorable roles in recent memory. He starred as "Marty McFly" in the *Back to the Future* trilogy and as "Alex Keaton" in the long running sitcom *Family Ties*. Recently, he has voiced animated lead characters in both *Stuart Little* movies and *Atlantis: The Lost Empire*. He and his wife, actress Tracy Pollan, founded the Michael J. Fox Foundation for Parkinson's Research to bring national attention and research dollars to help fight Parkinson's.

Tracy Pollan

Tracy Pollan met her future husband while acting the part of his girlfriend, "Ellen Reed," in the hit television sitcom, *Family Ties*. Tracy has been a prolific actress, starring in television movies such as *First to Die* and *Children of the Dark*. Tracy comes from the prestigious Actors' Studio. She is mother to their four children including twin girls.

Michael J. Fox and Tracy Pollan   73

THE MICHAEL J. FOX | **FOUNDATION FOR PARKINSON'S RESEARCH**

Founded in 2000, the Michael J. Fox Foundation for Parkinson's Research is dedicated to ensuring the development of a cure for Parkinson's disease within a decade through an aggressively funded research agenda. The foundation is committed to a major pursuit of all avenues of research, promising improved therapies and ultimately a cure for people living with Parkinson's disease. Enormous progress toward finding a cure has been made on many neurological fronts, and scientists' understanding of the brain and how this disease affects it has increased dramatically. The foundation seeks to hasten progress further by awarding grants that help guarantee that new and innovative research avenues are thoroughly funded and explored. More than $78 million in research has been funded to date, either directly or through partnerships.

"More than one million people in the United States—six million people worldwide—are living with Parkinson's disease, a chronic, degenerative neurological disorder characterized by symptoms that typically progress from mild tremors to complete physical incapacitation. In its final stages, Parkinson's leaves people unable to move, speak, or swallow. Despite modest advances in pharmaceutical and surgical therapies, there is no known cure at present.

The Michael J. Fox Foundation for Parkinson's Research was founded in 2000 with a single goal in mind—*to accelerate the development of a cure for Parkinson's disease.* Scientists believe that, with proper research funding, this goal is within reach. The Foundation has funded millions of dollars for Parkinson's research. The opportunity for therapeutic breakthroughs has never been greater, and advances in Parkinson's research are likely to contribute significantly to the understanding of other devastating neurological diseases such as Alzheimer's, Lou Gehrig's, and multiple sclerosis."

—*Michael J. Fox*

Each year when summer is fading and the kids are starting back at school, the Pollan family gather together over a hundred friends and family for an old-fashioned barn dance. It's a casual weekend in the New England countryside filled with fishing in ponds, hay rides, square dancing—a lot of great memories. Over the years, it's become a "can't miss" event in our family. At various times, both of us have taken a weekend off from filming and flown in just to make it.

On Saturday night there is a big potluck dinner that's always a lot of fun. The recipes we've included have been collected over the years from friends and family who introduced us to these wonderful dishes at the barn dance dinner. Enjoy!

MENU

Swing Your Partners, Swing Your Forks, It's Our Barn Dance Potluck

BEAN SALAD

KOREAN BARBECUE

BARN DANCE CHICKEN

OATMEAL COOKIES

© 2006 Michael J. Fox. Used with permission.

BEAN SALAD

Serves 8

Ingredients

★ 2 (14 ounce) cans black beans, drained and rinsed

★ 2 (14 ounce) cans corn, drained

★ 1 medium red onion chopped

★ ⅔ cup chopped cilantro

★ Italian salad dressing

Directions

1. In a bowl, mix together the all ingredients except the dressing. Add salad dressing to taste and mix well. Add additional cilantro if desired.

KOREAN BARBECUE

Serves 6 (using short ribs)
Serves 10–12 (using steak)

Ingredients

★ 1½–2 cups shoyu sauce or soy sauce
★ 2 tablespoons sugar
★ 2 tablespoons sesame oil
★ 1 tablespoon toasted sesame seeds
★ 6 cloves garlic, minced
★ 6 stalks (green portion) green onions, chopped
★ Freshly ground black pepper
★ 5 pounds cross-cut short ribs, or substitute
  flank steak or skirt steak

Directions

1. In a large bowl, combine all ingredients
   except the meat and mix well. Add the meat
   and marinate, turning occasionally, for
   approximately 1 hour.

2. Grill meat, preferably on a hibachi or other
   charcoal grill, until meat is done to your
   liking.

BARN DANCE CHICKEN

Serves 12

Ingredients

★ 1 cup ketchup
★ ¼ cup sherry vinegar
★ 1 teaspoon freshly ground black pepper
★ 2 chickens, each cut into 6 pieces, skin on
★ 3 pounds Vidalia onions, sliced thin
★ 2 tablespoons chopped fresh thyme

Directions

1. Combine ketchup, vinegar, and pepper. Pour over chicken pieces and allow to marinate overnight.

2. Preheat oven to 325°F.

3. Divide onions evenly between two roasting pans. Transfer chicken pieces on top of the onions, laying chicken skin side up and in one layer. Cover with any remaining marinade.

4. Cook for 1 hour and 15 minutes, and then increase heat to 475°F and cook for another 5 minutes.

OATMEAL COOKIES

Serves 12

Ingredients

★ 1 cup butter

★ 1 cup brown sugar

★ 1 cup white sugar

★ 1 egg

★ 1 cup flour

★ 1 teaspoon baking powder

★ ¼ teaspoon kosher salt

★ 1 teaspoon vanilla

★ ¾ cup coconut

★ 2¼ cups rolled oats

★ raisins (optional)

Directions

1. Preheat oven to 375°F.

2. In a mixer, cream together butter and sugars.

3. In a separate bowl, combine remaining ingredients, and add to creamed butter–sugar mixture, until just mixed.

4. Form dough into balls and press flat with fork. Bake for 15 minutes.

Brendan Fraser

The son of a Canadian travel executive who frequently moved his family, Brendan Fraser has been all over the world, and he credits his early exposure to London theater for inspiring his career. Brendan has appeared in both *Mummy* movies as well as a host of comic features including *George of the Jungle, Looney Tunes: Back in Action,* and *Blast from the Past.* He played the role of a district attorney in the Oscar-winning Paul Haggis film *Crash.* He is married to Afton and they have three children.

Afton Fraser

Afton Fraser is known to movie audiences as Afton Smith. She worked together with her husband-to-be on the 1997 movie *George of the Jungle.* The next year, Afton and Brendan tied the knot and started their family. Afton and Brendan share their birthday of December 3. Afton is also the author of *Hollywood Picks the Classics: A Guide for the Beginner and the Aficionado,* a guidebook for classic movies.

Brendan and Afton Fraser   83

P.S. ARTS

Dedicated to restoring arts education to public schools, P.S. ARTS provides comprehensive, skills-based, sequential classes in dance, drama, music, and visual arts to school children. The curriculum is aligned with California's Visual and Performing Arts Content Standards. Now in its 13th year, P.S. ARTS provides access to the arts through in-school programs to thousands of children in some of the most underserved neighborhoods in California. In addition, P.S. ARTS is active in the educational community, offering arts-related workshops for classroom teachers. The workshops are designed to inspire and instruct teachers how to integrate creative expression and the arts into the core curriculum.

"Afton and I support P.S. ARTS because we believe that the arts are essential and should be a part of every child's education. P.S. ARTS provides a comprehensive arts education program to 14,000 students in 25 schools. Once P.S. ARTS partners with a school, it never leaves, so the students get the arts at least once a week, year after year, until they graduate. We love the fact that P.S. ARTS serves the neediest children first—about 75% of the kids in their programs live below poverty level (currently a $19,500 household income for a family of four). We have been involved with the organization for three years and plan to continue our support until every child in the state of California (and beyond) has the opportunity to learn about visual arts, music, drama, and dance in their neighborhood public school. Kids need the arts!!"

—*Brendan Fraser*

We started having movie nights at our home to share our love of classic films with friends. Adding a dinner to match the theme of the movie made the evening more memorable and fun. Of course you can watch movies from any genre. They don't have to be old ones. Enjoy!

MENU

That's Amore— Our Italian Movie Night

BRUSCHETTA con ZUCCHINI SFRANTE

FRITO di MALANZANE FILANTI

ROASTED ZUCCHINI RISOTTO

PENNE with ROASTED FARMER'S MARKET VEGETABLES
AND ROASTED PEPPER SAUCE

POLLO en POTACCHIO

CROSTADA

BRUSCHETTA con ZUCCHINI SFRANTE
BRUSCHETTA with ZUCCHINI PURÉE AND SUN-DRIED TOMATOES

Serves 6

Ingredients

★ ¼ cup extra virgin olive oil

★ ¼ cup small onion, peeled and chopped

★ 2 medium zucchini, washed,
   ends removed, and coarsely chopped

★ 2 garlic cloves

★ 2 tablespoons chopped fresh basil

★ 2 tablespoons chopped fresh parsley

★ Kosher salt and freshly ground pepper

★ 6 thick slices of fresh Italian bread

★ 2 garlic cloves (to rub on bread)

★ 6 sun-dried tomatoes packed in oil,
   drained, and cut into strips (optional)

Directions

1. In a small sauté pan, gently heat 2 tablespoons olive oil. Add the onions and cook until soft and translucent. Add the zucchini, garlic, and herbs.

2. Cover the pan and cook over medium heat, stirring frequently, until zucchini falls apart completely. Season with salt and pepper.

3. Grill or lightly toast the bread slices. Rub with the garlic cloves and drizzle with remaining 2 tablespoons olive oil.

4. Spread the zucchini purée on the grilled bread. Garnish with sun-dried tomatoes (optional).

Brendan and Afton Fraser

FRITO DI MALANZANE FILANTI
EGGPLANT AND CHEESE SANDWICHES

Serves 6

Ingredients

- ★ 2 pounds ripe tomatoes, quartered
- ★ ½ cup olive oil, divided, plus more for frying sandwiches
- ★ 1 onion, sliced
- ★ 1 carrot, peeled and diced
- ★ 1 leek, cleaned and diced
- ★ 6 cloves garlic, chopped
- ★ 1 teaspoon chopped fresh thyme leaves
- ★ ¼ cup chopped fresh basil leaves
- ★ Kosher salt and freshly ground black pepper
- ★ 3 globe eggplants, sliced into rounds, salted and drained
- ★ 8 ounces fresh mozzarella, sliced
- ★ ½ cup sun-dried tomatoes, reconstituted and sliced
- ★ ½ cup flour for dredging
- ★ 2 eggs, beaten
- ★ ½ cup fine breadcrumbs
- ★ Olive oil for frying

Directions

1. Preheat oven to 350°F.

2. Prepare the sauce: toss the ripe tomatoes with 2 tablespoons olive oil. Season with salt and pepper. Roast in the oven until soft and tender, about 30 minutes. Remove from oven.

3. In a medium sauté pan, heat 2 tablespoons olive oil and sweat the onion over medium heat. Add the carrot, leek, and garlic and continue cooking until soft, about 10 minutes. Add the roasted tomatoes and the herbs. Simmer until the flavors come together, about 30 minutes. Remove from heat, purée and season with salt and pepper.

4. Prepare the sandwiches: season the eggplant slices with salt and pepper. Heat a large sauté pan with ¼ cup olive oil and cook, flipping once, until slices are tender. Drain on paper towels and allow to cool.

5. Assemble the sandwiches by layering mozzarella and sun-dried tomatoes between two eggplant slices. When all sandwiches have been made, dredge them in flour, then in the beaten eggs, then coat them with bread crumbs. Fry sandwiches in about ½ cup of olive oil until golden brown. Drain on paper towels and serve with the sauce.

ROASTED ZUCCHINI RISOTTO

Serves 2 to 4

Ingredients

★ 2 zucchini, diced

★ 1 tablespoon plus 2 tablespoons olive oil

★ Kosher salt and freshly ground black pepper

★ 1 clove garlic, smashed

★ ½ onion, diced

★ ½ cup Arborio rice

★ 2 cups chicken stock or vegetable stock

★ ¼ cup grated parmesan cheese

★ 2 tablespoons butter

★ 2 teaspoons fresh thyme leaves

Directions

1. Preheat oven to 425°F.

2. Toss the zucchini with 1 tablespoon olive oil, salt, and pepper and roast until tender, about 10 minutes. Remove from oven.

3. In a medium sauté pan, heat 2 tablespoons olive oil. Add onion and cook until tender, about 4 minutes. Add garlic and cook for 1 minute. Add rice and stir vigorously to coat with oil.

4. Add ½ cup stock and simmer until absorbed. Follow with more stock, in ½ cup increments, stirring until each addition is absorbed. Continue until the rice is cooked al dente, about 20 minutes total.

5. Stir in zucchini, cheese, butter, and thyme. Season with salt and pepper.

PENNE
WITH ROASTED FARMER'S MARKET VEGETABLES AND ROASTED PEPPER SAUCE

Serves 2 to 4

Ingredients

★ ½ pound fresh vegetables, cut into bite sized pieces
★ 2 tablespoons olive oil, divided
★ Kosher salt and freshly ground black pepper
★ 1 shallot, sliced
★ ½ cup white wine
★ ¼ cup chicken stock
★ ¼ cup cream (optional)
★ 1 red bell pepper, roasted, seeded, skinned, and sliced
★ ¼ cup chopped basil
★ ½ pound penne pasta

Directions

1. Preheat oven to 425°F. Start to bring a large pot of cold water to a boil.

2. Toss vegetables in 1 tablespoon olive oil and roast the vegetables until done, about 10 minutes. Remove from oven.

3. In a small sauté pan, heat remaining 1 tablespoon olive oil. Add shallots and cook until translucent. Add wine and reduce by half. Add stock and cream. Add peppers and basil, remove from heat, and purée. Season with salt and pepper.

4. When water boils, add 2 tablespoons salt and cook pasta according to package directions. Drain and toss with pepper sauce and roasted vegetables.

POLLO en POTACCHIO
CHICKEN in TOMATO SAUCE

Serves 2-4

Ingredients

* ★ ½ cup extra virgin olive oil
* ★ 1 onion, chopped
* ★ 1 sprig fresh rosemary, chopped
* ★ 1 pound ripe tomatoes, peeled, seeds removed, and chopped
* ★ Kosher salt
* ★ Pinch cayenne
* ★ 1 chicken, cut into six pieces
* ★ 6 tablespoons butter
* ★ 2 cloves garlic, crushed
* ★ 1 medium onion, thinly sliced
* ★ ½ cup dry white wine

Directions

1. Preheat oven to 325°F.

2. Prepare the sauce: heat ¼ olive oil in a heavy pan and sauté the chopped onion and rosemary gently until the onion is golden brown. Add the tomatoes and sprinkle with salt and cayenne. Bring to a gentle boil, lower heat to a simmer, and cook for 20 minutes.

3. Prepare the chicken: heat remaining ¼ cup olive oil and 4 tablespoons butter in a shallow heatproof pan or large sauté pan. Season the chicken with salt and pepper. Add garlic and chicken pieces to the pan and cook, turning once, until golden brown (about 5 minutes). When the garlic cloves are browned, discard them. Add the wine and continue cooking slowly, covered, until the chicken is tender (around 10 minutes).

4. Pour the sauce over the chicken, dot with remaining butter and cook in the oven until chicken is cooked through, approximately 20 minutes longer.

CROSTADA
FRESH FRUIT TART

Serves 10

Ingredients

Pastry:
- ★ 4 ounces unsalted butter
- ★ 2 cups all-purpose flour
- ★ 2 tablespoons sugar
- ★ 2 egg yolks
- ★ 2–4 tablespoons milk

Filling:
- ★ 1 cup sugar
- ★ 5 egg yolks
- ★ $\frac{2}{3}$ cup flour
- ★ 2 cups milk
- ★ 4 tablespoons cognac
- ★ 1 cup blanched almonds, finely chopped
- ★ 1 egg white
- ★ 3 cups fresh seasonal fruit (cherries, plums, peaches, nectarines, apricots, strawberries, raspberries, grapes, figs, or oranges)
- ★ 1 cup apricot jam for the glaze

Directions

1. Make the pastry: mix the flour and sugar and cut in the butter with a pastry cutter or in a food processor. Add the egg yolks and just enough milk to bind into a soft dough, stirring, and then briefly mixing by hand. Wrap in plastic wrap and chill for 1 hour.

2. Make the custard: In the bowl of a mixer, beat the sugar into the egg yolks until light and pale, then beat in the flour. In a heavy saucepan, bring the milk to a boil and pour slowly into the egg mixture, beating vigorously, until well blended. Pour mixture back into saucepan, stirring constantly, and return to a boil; reduce heat. Simmer 3 minutes longer, stirring occasionally so the custard does not burn. Stir in cognac and almonds and allow cool.

3. Preheat oven to 400°F.

4. Roll out the dough on a floured board with a floured rolling pin. Lift dough with the rolling pin and lay it gently into a 13-inch tart pan, pat it into place, and press into the sides. Trim the edges and prick it all over with a fork to prevent puffing. Bake for 10 minutes. Remove and brush with egg white to seal crust. Return to the oven for 5 to 10 minutes longer, or until it is a light golden color. Remove from oven and cool.

5. Spread the custard over the cooled crust. Top with as much fruit as you can fit, making an attractive pattern.

6. Melt the apricot jam in a saucepan with a few tablespoons of water and spoon it over the fruit.

Brendan and Afton Fraser   93

Rocco DiSpirito

Rocco DiSpirito began his culinary experience at age eleven in his mother Nicolina's kitchen in Queens. By the age of sixteen, DiSpirito entered the Culinary Institute of America. He graduated in 1986 and studied abroad at Jardin de Cygne in France. In 1997, DiSpirito opened Union Pacific in New York City's Gramercy Park as chef and owner. In 1999, DiSpirito was named *Food & Wine's* Best New Chef, and in 2000, *Gourmet* magazine called him "America's Most Exciting Young Chef." DiSpirito opened Rocco's 22nd Street in the summer of 2003 while cameras for NBC's *The Restaurant* watched and took notes. Later that summer, more than nine million viewers a week tuned in to see the ups and downs of DiSpirito's family-inspired eatery. The second series aired in the spring of 2004. His third book *5 Minute Flavor* (Scribner) was published in 2006, and he currently is working on a television show for A&E.

MAMA'S MEATBALLS

Serves 6

Ingredients

★ ⅓ cup chicken stock
★ ¼ cup diced yellow onions
★ 1 clove garlic, minced
★ ¼ cup fresh parsley, chopped fine
★ ½ pound ground beef
★ ½ pound ground pork
★ ½ pound ground veal
★ ⅓ cup plain bread crumbs
★ 2 eggs
★ ¼ cup Parmigiano-Reggiano cheese, grated
★ 1 teaspoon red pepper flakes
★ 1 teaspoon kosher salt
★ ¼ cup extra virgin olive oil
★ 3 to 6 cups of your favorite marinara sauce

Directions

1. Place the chicken stock, onion, garlic, and parsley in a blender or food processor and purée.

2. In a large bowl, combine the puréed stock mix, meat, bread crumbs, egg, cheese, red pepper flakes, and salt. Combine using hands until mixture is uniform, being careful not to overmix. Put a little olive oil on your hands and form mixture into balls a little larger than golf balls.

3. Pour about ½ inch of olive oil in 10-inch straight-sided sauté pan and heat over medium-high heat. Add the meatballs to the pan, working in batches if necessary, and brown meatballs, turning once. This should take about 10 to15 minutes.

4. While meatballs are browning, heat the marinara sauce in a large pot. Transfer the meatballs to the pot with the marinara sauce and simmer for 1 hour. Serve alone or over your favorite pasta.

Greg Grunberg

Greg Grunberg slides easily between television and feature work, appearing as "Matt Parkman" on the NBC fall series *Heroes*. He also had a role recently in *Mission Impossible III* opposite Tom Cruise. To television audiences he is probably best known for his role as "Eric Weiss" on the hit series *Alias*. For four seasons, he also portrayed "Sean Blumberg" on the WB series, *Felicity*. Greg started his career with several high profile commercials, one of which was so memorable that it landed him a spot on *The Tonight Show*.

Pediatric **Epilepsy** Project

OUR CHILDREN LOOKING TO US FOR HOPE

The Pediatric Epilepsy Project at UCLA was formed with several goals: to raise funds, provide financial support, and increase community awareness to help sustain the Division of Pediatric Neurology at UCLA. The foundation's mission is to improve the lives of children with neurological disorders by providing the best clinical care possible based on current knowledge. The UCLA program also conducts cutting edge clinical and basic science research that will advance the care of patients and give direction to others throughout the world. The nonprofit facilitates the development of faculty and trains the next generation of pediatric neurologists.

" A few words about my charity: PEP, the Pediatric Epilepsy Project to benefit the Division of Pediatric Neurology at UCLA.

Together with other parents who have children suffering from epilepsy and are also being treated at UCLA, I am behind a major fundraising effort to provide the funds needed to keep the Division of Pediatric Neurology at UCLA up and running. To do that, I have enlisted the help of every celebrity I could get my hands on to personally finger paint canvases and Gibson guitars to auction off to the public. We have turned the works of art into greeting card sets that are available to the public at *www.celebritycards.com*—check them out.

This is how it all came together: My son Jake has epilepsy. At first my wife Elizabeth and I had no idea how to handle it. After a year and a half with different doctors and several medications, we finally found success with the help of Dr. Sankar and the rest of the incredible medical staff at the Division of Pediatric Neurology at UCLA. They put our son on a combination of drugs, including Lamictal®, and he is now relatively seizure-free. He's doing great in every aspect of his life, and we couldn't be happier. Every child living with epilepsy deserves the same chance and treatment. The only thing UCLA is missing is the proper amount of funding to continue its heroic work. It became my mission to raise money for them.

In addition to purchasing this beautiful cookbook, if you would like to help kids with epilepsy live a seizure-free life, go to *www. celebritycards.com* to purchase a pack of hand-painted celebrity greeting cards by some of your favorite actors, musicians, and athletes. Either way, you are helping to give children with epilepsy a fighting chance."

—*Greg Grunberg*

addy's Mexican Fiesta is what my boys call it when I prepare Mexican food. It all goes back to my own childhood, when my mother would make her famous tamale pie and I was one of the lucky recipients of her efforts. Family gatherings and the memories that come out of it are the real key to success with this meal. The food is all easy enough to make and very satisfying— a definite guilty pleasure. In the interest of good eating, I'm even sharing the secret ingredient in my guacamole recipe. There's even a recipe that lets your guests do all the work and lets you have some time off to enjoy them! Enjoy!

Holy Tamale!
It's Our Cinco de Mayo Fiesta

MO'BETTA MOJITO

GRUN-A-MOLE

MY MEXICAN RICE

MOM'S FAMOUS TAMALE PIE

RAISING THE TACO BAR

GOOD KARMA FLAN

MO'BETTA MOJITO

Serves 4

Ingredients

★ 4 tablespoons cane sugar,
  plus more to rim glass if desired
★ 4 cups ice
★ 6 ounces light rum
★ 10 to 12 mint sprigs
★ 6 tablespoons freshly squeezed lime
  juice
★ Club soda
★ 4 slices lime

Directions

1. Moisten the rims of 4 funky glasses
   with lime and dip into cane sugar.
   Set aside.

2. Place ice in a beverage shaker and
   add in the rum. Break up half of the
   mint leaves and add to the shaker
   along with the lime juice and sugar.
   Shake well and serve over ice in
   glasses. Top off each glass with a
   splash of club soda and garnish
   with a slice of lime and a sprig of
   mint.

"GRUN-A-MOLE"
GUACAMOLE

"Everyone has his or her own version of the classic Mexican dip, but mine has a secret ingredient that you are just going to have to taste to appreciate."

Serves 12 to 24

Ingredients
* ★ 12 jumbo, ripe avocados, halved and pits removed
* ★ 1 pint salsa (store bought, your call)
* ★ 1 finely chopped white onion
* ★ 2 tablespoons freshly squeezed lemon juice
* ★ Kosher salt
* ★ 2 tablespoons hot sauce (*hot*, live a little)
* ★ 1 tablespoon brown sugar (trust me on this)

Directions

1. Scoop the avocado flesh from the skin and smash in a wooden bowl. Fold in the salsa, onions, lemon juice, salt, and brown sugar. Slowly add the hot sauce to taste, but don't be afraid to give it a good kick.

2. Sit back and take all the credit. You must divide into two bowls, placing them far apart, or there will be some elbows thrown and severe double dipping until all the guacamole is devoured.

MY MEXICAN RICE

(which isn't really mine . . . I stole this recipe, but I love it.)
"This dish could stand on it's own as a meal. Make tons of it, because you
 can enjoy it the next morning with your eggs (clothing optional)."

Serves 8

Ingredients

★ 2 tablespoons lard, or substitute vegetable oil
★ ½ cup ground pork
★ ¼ pound chorizo, sliced into ¼-inch pieces
★ ½ cup chopped onions
★ ¼ cup chopped bell peppers
★ 2 teaspoons minced garlic
★ 2 cups long-grain rice
★ 1 large tomato, peeled, seeded, and chopped
★ 4 cups chicken stock
★ 1 teaspoon kosher salt
★ ½ teaspoon saffron
★ 1½ teaspoons chopped fresh oregano leaves
★ 1 teaspoon chopped fresh cilantro leaves
★ ¼ cup chopped green onions

Directions

1. In a nonstick saucepan, heat the lard over medium heat.
   Add the pork and cook, stirring frequently, until cooked
   through, about 5 minutes. Add the sausage slices and cook,
   stirring, for 1 minute. Add the onions and bell peppers, and
   cook, stirring, until soft, about 3 minutes. Add the garlic and
   cook for 30 seconds. Add the rice and cook, stirring, for 1
   minute. Add the tomatoes and cook, stirring, for 1 minute.

2. Add the stock, salt, and saffron, and stir well. Bring to a boil,
   then lower the heat to simmer, cover, and cook undisturbed
   until all the liquid is absorbed, about 20 minutes.

3. Remove from the heat and let sit, covered, for 10 minutes.
   Uncover and fluff the rice with a fork. Add the oregano and
   cilantro, and stir to incorporate. Serve in a decorative bowl
   and garnish with the green onions. Serve immediately.

MOM'S FAMOUS TAMALE PIE

*"Making this dish is almost as much fun as eating it. I grew up on this stuff.
My mother would let us crumble and layer and get our hands in there. Enjoy!"*

Serves 8

Ingredients

★ 12 large prepared beef tamales
★ 4 cups grated Mexican cheese
  (Cojita or other type)
★ 3 small cans of sliced black olives
★ 3 small cans of tomato juice
★ 2 large chopped sweet onions
★ 3 large cans of sweet corn, drained
★ 2 tablespoons hot sauce
  (HOT, live a little more)

Directions

1. Preheat oven to 275°F.

2. In a large, deep baking dish, break up 2 to 3 of the tamales, forming a layer at the bottom. Follow that with a layer of cheese, then a layer of olives, then onions, and then corn. Repeat this layering process until you run out of ingredients. Make sure that you finish with a thick layer of cheese.

2. Using the dowel end of a wooden spoon, poke several holes through the layers. Pour the tomato juice onto the assembled layers, being sure to pour some juice into holes.

3. Bake for 30 minutes, until bubbly.

RAISING THE TACO BAR

"Nothing is more fun and comforting than making your own tacos at a party.
Dig in and have fun!"

Ingredients

★ Warm flour tortillas
★ Warm corn tortillas
★ Warm hard taco shells
★ Cooked ground chicken
★ Cooked ground beef
★ Cooked pulled pork
★ Sweet canned corn, drained
★ Tons of great shredded Mexican cheeses
★ Tons of melted nacho cheese
   (yes, the ballpark kind)
★ Chopped sweet Maui onions
★ Large bowl of shredded lettuce
★ Several different salsas
★ Several different hot sauces

Directions

1. Lay out the taco bar on a table or counter. Arrange items on different levels. Try to keep heated items covered so they will be warm for seconds and thirds. Trust me, your guests will be back for more.

GOOD KARMA FLAN

Serves 12

Ingredients

* ★ 1½ cups sugar
* ★ ½ cup boiling water
* ★ 2 cups half-and-half
* ★ 1 cup heavy cream
* ★ 1 cup sugar
* ★ 4 strips orange zest (each about 2 inches long and ½ inch wide), pith removed
* ★ 12 jumbo egg yolks
* ★ ¼ cup tawny port

Directions

1. Make the caramelized sugar syrup: place ½ cup sugar in a medium-size heavy pot (not iron), over moderately low heat, and allow to melt and caramelize to a rich golden brown. Do not stir the sugar as it melts, but do shake the pot from time to time. Add the boiling water, stirring briskly with a wooden spoon to dissolve the caramelized sugar. Simmer uncovered, 8 to 10 minutes, until the syrup has the consistency of maple syrup. Reserve 2 tablespoons of the caramelized syrup for the flan; pour the balance into a chilled, well-buttered, shallow, fluted 2-quart mold. Set the mold in the freezer while preparing the flan.

2. Preheat the oven to 325°F.

3. Make the flan: combine the half-and-half, heavy cream, and 1 cup sugar in a large heavy saucepan. Add in the orange zest and bring to a simmer over moderately low heat, stirring now and then; blend in the 2 tablespoons of reserved caramelized syrup.

4. In a bowl, beat the egg yolks until frothy. Slowly blend 1 cup of the hot cream mixture into the yolks, stir back into pan, and heat, stirring constantly for 1 minute, until it lightly coats the back of a spoon. Remove from the heat and mix in the port. Strain through a fine sieve, and pour into the prepared mold.

5. Set the mold in a shallow baking pan and pour in enough hot water to come halfway up the mold. Bake uncovered for 1½ hours or until a toothpick inserted near the center of the flan comes out clean. Remove from the oven and the water bath; cool for 1 hour, then refrigerate for 4 to 5 hours until firm.

6. To invert the flan, dip the mold quickly in hot water, then turn out on a dessert plate with a turned up rim; the caramel syrup will come cascading down over the flan. Don't worry if the flan cracks—it will still be creamy and luscious. Cut into slim wedges, if possible, or scoop out, and serve.

Greg Grunberg 109

Anne Hathaway

Anne Hathaway is best known as "Princess Mia Thermopolis" in the *Princess Diaries* films. Recently, her schedule has been busy with several more movie roles, including starring opposite Meryl Streep in *The Devil Wears Prada*, and in the Ang Lee drama *Brokeback Mountain*. She is also known for a starring role in *Ella Enchanted*. Anne was honored with a 2002 Teen Choice award as "Best Actress in a Comedy" for her breakout role in the *Princess Diaries*.

Anne Hathaway   111

Lollipop
THEATER NETWORK

Lollipop Theater Network (LOLLIPOP) is dedicated to bringing the laughter and magic of movies to children confined to hospitals nationwide due to chronic or life-threatening illnesses. LOLLIPOP is the first and only organization of its kind to work with the full collaboration of the leading motion picture studios to bring current G, PG, and PG-13 film releases into hospitals for group and bedside screenings on an ongoing basis. We all believe hope and laughter are key ingredients in having the strength to fight and to cope with hospitalization. LOLLIPOP literally rolls out the red carpet for these very deserving children and provides special movie tickets, memorabilia, and visits by the stars of the film. Our goal is to provide a brief escape from the illnesses and daily medical treatments these children face and to create a sense of normalcy in their lives and the lives of their families.

"I support Lollipop Theater Network because I believe in the importance of entertainment. It is not an overstatement to say that the arts and entertainment are among the greatest unifiers in our world today, and are among the few things that still make us laugh and smile. Lollipop not only serves to uphold that but also focuses on the individuals who need those laughs the most. There are few greater joys in life than to be able to make someone's day during troubled times, and Lollipop does just that."

—*Anne Hathaway*

I chose a Mediterranean theme for my recipes simply because I was on a Mediterranean cruise when I was asked to participate, and the food was making me feel so good. Everything is absolutely delicious with unique ingredients. Best of all, it is simple to prepare, which is a prerequisite for getting me in the kitchen.

Anne Hath a Way with Mediterranean Cuisine

LOBSTER MANGO SALAD

MEDITERRANEAN CHICKEN

STUFFED AUBERGINES

BUCATINI A LA POMODORO AL FORNO

MEDITERRANEAN BAKED WHITE FISH

STUFFED PEACHES

LOBSTER MANGO SALAD

Serves 6

Ingredients

★ 1 teaspoon coconut milk
★ Juice of 1 lime
★ Zest of ½ lime
★ ⅛ teaspoon red sweet chili sauce
★ 4 shallots
★ 2 cloves garlic
★ 1 tablespoon pickled ginger
★ ¼ cup fresh dill
★ 2 tablespoons fish sauce
★ 3 lobsters, about 3 pounds each, or substitute crayfish
★ ⅔ cup peeled and diced mango
★ ½ cucumber, peeled, seeded, and sliced thin
★ 3 cups salad mix

Directions

1. Combine coconut milk, lime juice and zest, chili sauce, shallots, garlic, ginger, dill, and fish sauce in a blender and blend well. Pour mixture into a saucepan and bring to a boil. Reduce heat and simmer for 20 minutes. Allow to cool.

2. Fill a large pot with water, cover and bring to a boil. Immerse lobsters. Place lid on pot and boil for 12 minutes. Remove lobsters from water and allow to cool.

3. Separate lobster tails from bodies and reserve bodies for another use. Slice each tail in half lengthwise, remove meat, and chop meat into large pieces. Remove meat from claws. Place meat into a bowl, add coconut mixture and mango and gently toss. Refrigerate until ready to serve.

4. Clean lobster tail shells and arrange on a platter. If desired, fill shells with lobster salad or serve plated with a dill garnish.

Anne Hathaway   115

MEDITERRANEAN CHICKEN

Serves 6

Ingredients

★ 6 boneless, skinless chicken cutlets (3 whole breasts)

★ ¾ cup red wine vinegar

★ ¾ cup extra virgin olive oil

★ 3 garlic cloves, smashed

★ 2 tablespoons minced fresh oregano leaves

★ 2 tablespoons capers

★ ⅓ cup dried apricots

★ ⅓ cup pitted prunes

★ 1 handful pitted green or black olives

★ 3 bay leaves

★ Kosher salt and freshly ground black pepper

★ ¾ cup white wine

★ ½ cup brown sugar

★ 6 cups salad mix

Directions

1. Place chicken in a large baking dish. In a bowl, combine vinegar, oil, garlic, oregano, capers, apricots, prunes, olives, and bay leaves and season with salt and pepper. Mix well. Pour mixture over chicken breasts and place, covered, in refrigerator. Allow chicken to marinate for 4 hours or overnight.

2. Preheat oven to 350°F.

3. Remove chicken dish from refrigerator and discard bay leaves. Pour wine over the top of chicken and sprinkle with sugar.

4. Place dish in oven and bake for 20 to 30 minutes, until chicken is cooked through.

5. Serve chicken breasts on a bed of rice or salad.

STUFFED AUBERGINES
STUFFED EGGPLANTS

Serves 6

Ingredients

★ 3 large eggplants with stems (4 to 5 pounds), halved lengthways
★ 2 tablespoons extra virgin olive oil
★ 2 red onions, finely chopped
★ 3 garlic cloves, finely chopped
★ 2 cups chopped fresh plum tomatoes
★ 1 tablespoon tomato paste
★ 1 cup fresh basil leaves
★ Kosher salt and freshly ground black pepper
★ 8 ounces (2 balls) fresh mozzarella, sliced thin

Directions

1. Preheat oven to 350°F.

2. Score eggplant flesh in a criss-cross pattern; avoid piercing the skin. In a large sauté pan, heat 1 tablespoon olive oil over medium heat. Place eggplant halves in the pan, flesh down, and cook until softened, about 4 minutes. Flip and cook for 2 more minutes. Remove from heat and cool.

3. In a separate sauté pan, heat 1 tablespoon olive oil and cook onions over low heat until soft, around 4 minutes. Add garlic, tomatoes, and tomato paste and cook for 3 minutes.

4. Carefully scoop flesh from eggplants and reserve skins. Chop eggplant flesh and add to the tomato mixture. Stir in basil and season with salt and pepper. Stuff reserved skins with mixture. Top with mozzarella slices and bake for 10 minutes or until cheese has melted.

BUCATINI A LA POMODORO AL FORNO

Serves 6

Ingredients

★ 2 pints cherry tomatoes, halved

★ 2 garlic cloves, smashed

★ 3 tablespoons extra virgin olive oil

★ 1 tablespoon good-quality dried oregano
   or 2 tablespoons chopped fresh oregano leaves

★ 1 cup fresh bread crumbs (made by
   blending crusty bread in food processor)

★ 1 pound package dried bucatini or spaghetti

★ 2 tablespoons kosher salt, plus more for seasoning

★ Freshly ground black pepper

★ Finely grated pecorino cheese

Directions

1. Preheat oven to 350°F.

2. Place tomato halves on a baking dish.
   Add garlic, olive oil, oregano, and bread
   crumbs and mix. Place baking dish in oven
   and roast until tomatoes are cooked, about
   25 minutes. Remove pan from oven and
   discard garlic. Crush tomatoes with a fork.
   Season to taste with salt and pepper.

3. While tomatoes are cooking, bring a
   large pot of cold water to a boil. Add 2
   tablespoons salt. Cook pasta until al dente,
   normally ½ minute less than cooking time
   on package. Drain, mix in tomato mixture,
   and serve immediately. Top with pecorino
   cheese.

Anne Hathaway

MEDITERRANEAN BAKED WHITE FISH

"This is a great recipe for baked whole fish. There are no strict rules or ingredients, so be creative."

Serves 6

Ingredients

* ★ 6 small sea bream or other fish (1 pound each) or 3 red snapper or other fish (1½ pounds each), gilled, gutted, and scaled, with heads on
* ★ 12 stalks fresh herbs, such as parsley, dill, basil, and oregano
* ★ 2 lemons, sliced
* ★ Sea salt
* ★ Freshly ground black pepper
* ★ Extra virgin olive oil

Directions

1. Preheat oven to 350°F.

2. Wash fish under cold running water and pat dry with paper towels.

3. Stuff each fish cavity with herbs and lemon and lay on a baking dish. Season well with salt and pepper and drizzle with olive oil.

4. Place in oven. Bake until just cooked, about 15 minutes for small fish and 20 minutes for larger fish. The flesh should be moist and easily peel away from the bone. Serve whole on a platter, or filet and place on individual plates.

Alternate cooking methods:

* Grill fish. Carefully flip halfway through cooking.

* Bake fish on a layer of precooked small potatoes (sliced about ½ inch thick), red peppers, and chicken stock seasoned with saffron.

* Bake fish in white wine.

STUFFED PEACHES

Serves 6

Ingredients

★ 3 large ripe peaches
★ 4 tablespoons butter, divided
★ ¾ cup crushed amaretti cookies
★ 1 large egg, beaten
★ 2 tablespoons amaretto (optional)
★ 2 tablespoons brown sugar, divided
★ 1 tablespoon ground almonds

Directions

1. Preheat oven to 350°F.

2. Rinse, halve, and pit peaches. Scoop out and reserve half of the flesh from each peach half.

3. Place peaches hollow side facing up, in a shallow baking dish greased with 1 tablespoon butter.

4. Mash reserved peach flesh. Cream 2 tablespoons butter with 1 tablespoon sugar and add to peach flesh. Mix in crushed cookies, egg, and amaretto. Stuff each peach half with ⅙ of the mixture.

5. Divide remaining tablespoon butter into 6 pieces and place one piece on top of each stuffed peach. Sprinkle each half with remaining brown sugar and ground almonds. Bake, uncovered, for 20 to 30 minutes or until peaches are softened and brown on top.

Paige Hemmis

As one of the featured designers on *Extreme Makeover: Home Edition*, Paige Hemmis may be an unlikely vision on a construction site, but she is an accomplished carpenter, skilled homebuilder, and savvy businesswoman. She came to television through auditioning to win tools on a show called *Monster House.* She appeared on the Christmas episode and was discovered by the producers of *Extreme Makeover: Home Edition.*

Working in partnership with low-income families to build decent homes they can afford to buy, Habitat for Humanity helps to break the cycle of poverty and hopelessness. More than one million people worldwide currently live in affordable houses thanks to Habitat for Humanity. But the need is still great. Over five million American families have worst-case housing needs, forced to endure overcrowded conditions and houses with severe physical deficiencies. While the number of families in poverty is growing, the number of affordable rental units is shrinking. Substandard housing can endanger the health and safety of its occupants, erode their hope and self-worth, and impair their children's ability to succeed in school. That's why Habitat for Humanity exists: to give families a better future.

"I support Habitat for Humanity because I see firsthand what a home means to a family, especially to children. A home is the heartbeat of your life, where you develop your sense of self. It's where dreams begin. The Habitat Partner Families come from sub-poverty level housing and discover a new life filled with security and possibility. As first-time homeowners they get an added sense of accomplishment and self-esteem having participated in the building of their homes. I am blessed to make my living building homes and changing lives every week and I am honored to work with Habitat, an organization that changes lives every single day all over the world."

—*Paige Hemmis*

This meal has been a crowd pleaser in my home on many occasions. Be warned: It's *not* light—it's for those *tough* men and women out there who aren't afraid to pick up a fork like it's a 2 × 4 and get to work. It will leave you and your guests happy, satisfied, and full. It will give them the energy to tackle the most difficult of projects and inspire them to take on more than they thought they could. Don't be surprised if they strap on a tool belt, exchange that fork for a hammer, and begin building a house.

MENU

Fork Raising for Building Appetites— Some Crowd Pleasers

DOOR KNOB SWEET POTATOES

NUTS AND BOLTS SALAD

SWEET AND SOUR "HOUSE" SALAD

TUFF STUFFED MUSHROOMS

FIXER-UPPER FISH

MUD CAKES

DOOR KNOB SWEET POTATOES

Serves 6

Ingredients

* ★ 1 pound sweet potatoes
* ★ 1 egg, beaten
* ★ 1 small onion, minced
* ★ 1 tablespoon milk
* ★ 1 tablespoon butter
* ★ ¾ teaspoon grated, peeled fresh ginger root
* ★ 2 tablespoons unbleached white flour
* ★ 1 tablespoon chopped fresh parsley
* ★ Pinch of cayenne pepper
* ★ Kosher salt and freshly ground black pepper to taste
* ★ ¼ cup vegetable oil
* ★ 2 cups whole wheat bread crumbs

Directions

1. Peel, cut up and cook the sweet potatoes in boiling water, just as you would to make mashed potatoes. Then mash them up adding milk until you get a good, doughy, mashed potato consistency.

2. Mix the mashed sweet potatoes together with beaten egg, minced onion, milk, butter, ginger, flour, parsley, cayenne, salt, and pepper.

3. Heat the oil in a heavy pan on medium heat. Put the breadcrumbs on a flat surface on plastic wrap or waxed paper. Form 1½ inch balls of the sweet potato mixture with a spoon or fingers. Roll each ball through the breadcrumbs, covering completely. Place the balls in the pan with hot oil, rolling them around occasionally to brown entire ball. When golden brown, transfer and drain on paper towels. Serve hot.

NUTS AND BOLTS SALAD
GREEN BEAN AND TOMATO SALAD

Serves 6

Ingredients

★ 1½ pounds fresh green beans, ends trimmed
★ Juice of 1 lemon
★ 3 tablespoons vegetable oil
★ 1 teaspoon kosher salt
★ 2 garlic cloves, minced
★ 20 small grape tomatoes

Directions

1. Cut beans diagonally into bite-sized pieces. Bring a pot of salted water to a boil and cook for 10 minutes. Drain beans and cool.

2. In a bowl, blend lemon juice, oil, salt, and garlic. Add the cooled green beans and grape tomatoes. Stir until coated.

SWEET AND SOUR "HOUSE" SALAD

Serves 8

Ingredients

★ ½ cup balsamic vinegar

★ ¼ cup olive oil

★ ¼ cup spiced mustard

★ ¼ cup honey

★ Kosher salt and freshly ground black pepper

★ 4 cups (1 bag) mixed baby field greens

★ 6 large mushrooms, sliced

★ ¼ cup toasted pine nuts

★ ½ cup dried cranberries

★ ¼ pound mozzarella cheese, grated

★ 1 pint small grape tomatoes

Directions

1. Make vinaigrette: combine vinegar, olive oil, mustard, and honey in a bowl and whisk together. Season with salt and pepper.

2. Empty the mixed baby field greens into a large salad bowl. Add remaining ingredients and toss with vinaigrette.

TUFF STUFFED MUSHROOMS

Serves 6

Ingredients

- ★ 18 large mushrooms, brushed clean, stems removed and reserved
- ★ ⅓ cup extra virgin olive oil
- ★ Juice of ½ lemon
- ★ 2 large garlic cloves, minced
- ★ ⅓ cup pine nuts, chopped
- ★ ⅓ cup bread crumbs (whole wheat or Italian bread)
- ★ ½ teaspoon red pepper flakes
- ★ Kosher salt and freshly ground black pepper

Directions

1. Preheat oven to 400°F.

2. Grease a shallow baking dish with some of the olive oil. Dip mushrooms into lemon juice, place in pan stem side up, making sure they fit tightly in the dish to keep the caps from overturning.

3. Finely dice the mushroom stems. Heat oil in a sauté pan over medium heat and cook chopped stems with the garlic, until the garlic turns golden. Stir in the pine nuts, bread crumbs, and red pepper flakes. Season with salt and pepper. Remove from heat and allow the mixture cool.

4. Fill the mushroom caps with stuffing and bake, uncovered, for 15 to 20 minutes.

FIXER-UPPER FISH

Serves 6

Ingredients

- ★ ½ cup extra virgin olive oil
- ★ 6 cloves garlic, minced
- ★ Pinch of cayenne
- ★ 2 teaspoons ground cumin seeds
- ★ 1 teaspoon ground coriander seeds
- ★ 3 cups of whole wheat bread crumbs
- ★ ½ cup chopped fresh basil
- ★ Kosher salt and freshly ground black pepper
- ★ 2 pounds firm white fish fillets
- ★ 2 medium tomatoes, chopped
- ★ ½ cup chopped fresh parsley
- ★ Juice of 2 lemons

Directions

1. Preheat oven to 350°F.

2. In a large skillet, heat the oil over medium heat. Add the garlic and cook until golden but not burned, about 1 minute. Add the cayenne, cumin, and coriander. Add the bread crumbs, continuously stirring, until the crumbs are golden brown and slightly crispy. Add the chopped basil, season with salt and pepper, stir until blended, and remove from the heat.

3. Rinse the fish fillets in cold water and place them, skin side down, in an oiled baking dish. Season with salt and pepper and distribute the chopped tomatoes evenly over the fish. Sprinkle on garlic and parsley. Lightly sprinkle the lemon juice over everything. Completely cover the fish with the bread crumb mixture.

4. Bake, uncovered, for 20 minutes.

MUD CAKES

Serves 8

Ingredients

★ 2 eggs

★ ¾ cup sugar

★ 1 teaspoon pure vanilla extract

★ ½ cup butter, melted

★ ¾ cup Ghirardelli® Sweet Ground Chocolate & Cocoa

★ ⅔ cup all-purpose flour

★ ¼ teaspoon baking powder

★ ¼ teaspoon salt

★ 1 cup Ghirardelli® Double or Semi-Sweet Chocolate Chips

★ Nonstick spray

★ Optional toppings: caramel sauce, vanilla ice cream, and powdered sugar

Directions

1. Preheat oven to 350° F.

2. In a bowl, whisk together eggs, sugar, vanilla, and butter.

3. In a separate bowl, sift together ground chocolate, flour, baking powder, and salt. Stir into egg mixture, and then stir in chips.

4. Spray the inside of individual cupcake pans with a nonstick spray. Fill each with batter, about ¾ of the way to the top. Bake 17 minutes.

5. While the cakes are still hot, turn one pan upside down onto a large plate. Carefully remove the pan, trying to keep the cupcake intact. Be very careful not to break the cupcake, as the inside is not completely done and will begin oozing out. If desired, serve with a scoop of ice cream, a light dusting of powdered sugar and a zigzag of caramel topping.

Watch as your guests take a fork to the cake and watch their surprise as the molten lava oozes from within. Yum!!!

Ron Howard

Ron Howard has worked in every aspect of the entertainment industry, from acting to producing to his current status as one of the world's top directors. Ron grew up on television with legendary roles on America's favorite shows such as *The Andy Griffith Show* and *Happy Days*. As a director, Ron has helmed major studio releases including *The Da Vinci Code, A Beautiful Mind, How the Grinch Stole Christmas,* and *Missing*. He has been married to his high school sweetheart Cheryl since 1975 and they have four children.

BOYS & GIRLS CLUBS
OF AMERICA

The Positive Place for Kids—that's what Boys & Girls Clubs have been to American kids for 100 years. Clubs serve some 4.6 million young people ages six to eighteen, with more than 3,900 locations across the country and on military bases around the world. Boys & Girls Clubs offer engaging programs and activities that build life skills. Every day, Clubs promote and enhance the development of young people by instilling a sense of competence, usefulness and belonging. In every community, Clubs are a safe place to learn and grow—all while having fun. Celebrating its national Centennial in 2006, Boys & Girls Clubs have inspired and enabled generations of young people, especially those who need it the most, to realize their full potential.

"The Boys & Girls Clubs of America have consistently advanced their programs and provided truly constructive activities for kids across the country. As cliché as it sounds, our young ones are our future, and we must invest in that future."

—*Ron Howard*

After a hard day on the set, we like to come home, relax, and whip up a quick and easy dinner. But just because it's easy to make doesn't mean it has to be bland or boring. Our palate goes to zesty Italian. We like to enjoy Tofu Marinara because it is one of the few guiltless dishes that actually makes me smile when I sit down to dig in. On a nutritional level, all but a few of us are doing ourselves a favor with this one, and yet, when prepared well, it's tasty, satisfying, and fun.

Lights, Camera, Dinner

BREAD AND DIPPING SAUCE

ROCKET SALAD

TOFU MARINARA

MAPLE COFFEE

STRAWBERRIES AND CHOCOLATE

BREAD
AND
DIPPING SAUCE

★ 1 loaf Ciabatta bread

Ingredients
★ Olive oil
★ Balsamic vinegar
★ Black Italian olives, diced
★ Garlic
★ Salt and pepper
★ Oregano
★ Basil
★ Red pepper flakes

Directions

1. Chop the black olives and mix in with the olive oil and vinegar, add minced garlic, oregano, basil, and salt and pepper to taste. If you like the zip, add a pinch of red pepper flakes. Let it sit for a while to let the flavors meld before serving.

Take hunks of bread and dip and enjoy.

Ron Howard

ROCKET SALAD

Serves 4

Ingredients

★ 3 tablespoons red wine vinegar

★ 9 tablespoons olive oil

★ ½ teaspoon kosher salt

★ ½ teaspoon freshly ground pepper

★ 4 cups arugula, washed and dried

★ 2 ounces parmesan cheese

Directions

1. Make vinaigrette: in a bowl or jar, combine vinegar, olive oil, salt, and pepper, and mix thoroughly.

2. Place arugula in a bowl and toss with vinaigrette.

3. Use a vegetable peeler and shave cheese on top.

TOFU MARINARA

Serves 4

Ingredients

★ 2 tablespoons olive oil

★ 2 cloves garlic

★ 1 small onion, chopped

★ ½ pound firm tofu,
  sliced into 4 pieces

★ 1 large can (32 ounces) crushed tomatoes

★ 1 teaspoon oregano

★ 1 teaspoon Italian parsley

★ Kosher salt and freshly ground
  black pepper

★ ½ cup red wine, optional

★ 1 box spaghetti cooked al dente
  (or 1 medium spaghetti squash,
  halved and seeded and roasted)

Directions

1. In a medium pot, heat oil over medium heat. Sauté the garlic and ½ of the onion. Add the tofu and cook for a few minutes, browning slightly. Remove tofu from pan and set aside.

2. Add tomatoes to pan. Add the herbs, remaining onion and season with salt and pepper. Add wine if you want. Cook for 15 minutes and then return the tofu to the pan. Cook for another 15 to 20 minutes.

3. Cook pasta till al dente. Divide pasta on plates and cover with sauce and tofu.

4. If desired you can replace spaghetti with spaghetti squash. Place squash halves cut side down on a cookie sheet and cook for 30 minutes, until tender. Remove from heat, cool and scrape out flesh with fork. Divide on plates as you would spaghetti.

Ron Howard 145

MAPLE COFFEE

Serves 4

Ingredients

★ 4 cups freshly brewed Arabica coffee, or substitute other favorite coffee

★ 2 cups steamed milk

★ 4 tablespoons maple syrup

Directions

1. Mix coffee with milk and add maple syrup to desired sweetness. Serve hot.

STRAWBERRIES AND CHOCOLATE

Serves 4

Ingredients

★ 2 pints of strawberries, washed, hulled and sliced

★ 1 (3½ ounces) bar Noir de Noir® Intense 70% Chocolate Bars, or substitute other favorite chocolate

★ 3 tablespoons heavy cream

★ Dash of vanilla extract

★ 2 cups whipped cream

Directions

1. In a saucepan, melt chocolate with the cream and vanilla.

2. Divide strawberries onto 4 plates, drizzle generously with the chocolate sauce and top with large dollops of whipped cream.

Jane Kaczmarek

Jane Kaczmarek is one of a long line of talented actors to come out of the Yale School of Drama. Television audiences best know Jane for her portrayal as "Lois" in *Malcolm in the Middle*, a role that has earned her nominations for seven consecutive Emmy awards, as well as numerous Golden Globe and SAG Awards and has won the American Comedy Award and the Television Critic's Awards for two consecutive years, the first woman to receive such an honor. Jane will next be seen on the ABC comedy *Help Me, Help You* opposite Ted Danson. Jane met Bradley Whitford on a blind date arranged by a college friend. They married in 1992 and have three children: Frances, George, and Mary Louisa.

Bradley Whitford

Bradley Whitford, a classically trained stage actor who has received critical acclaim for his roles in theater, film, and television, quickly gained overnight fame as the sarcastic yet vulnerable Josh Lyman on NBC's *The West Wing*. His performance has earned him a 2001 Emmy Award as well as Golden Globe Award nominations in 2001 and 2002. An alumnus of the Juilliard Theater Center, Bradley is one of the few actors working successfully and simultaneously in theater, film, and television and has become one of Hollywood's most sought-after talents. Bradley's current project is *Studio 60 on The Sunset Strip*. The highly anticipated NBC drama re-teams Whitford with Aaron Sorkin and focuses on a behind-the-scenes look at a fictional sketch-comedy TV show.

Jane Kaczmarek and Bradley Whitford 149

CLOTHES
OFF OUR BACK

Clothes Off Our Back® is an organization that hosts charity auctions showcasing today's hottest celebrity attire. Items are put up for bid to the public, with proceeds going to benefit children's charities. Clothes Off Our Back was founded by actors and philanthropists Jane Kaczmarek and Bradley Whitford, whose efforts, along with those of their celebrity and designer friends, have helped improve the lives of many across the globe. Every year, Clothes Off Our Back picks different children's charities as beneficiaries. Organizations such as UNICEF's efforts in Darfur, Cure Autism Now, Half the Sky and the Children's Defense Fund have been recipients of the auction and fundraising proceeds.

"Clothes Off Our Back was started as a way to share our good fortune by selling celebrity award show clothes online for children's charities. Brad and I both grew up in Wisconsin and share the Midwest sensibility of not wasting things. There are so many clothes in Hollywood that will never be worn again and so many children in need, that it seemed like a perfect union."

—*Jane Kaczmarek*

When it comes to cooking, our favorite recipes have one basic philosophy: combinations of delicious ingredients that are wonderful comfort foods. On those rare rainy nights in Los Angeles, we can't wait to get into the kitchen, put on our aprons, and make one of the following recipes.

It Sometimes Rains in Southern California

WARM PEAR SALAD

SLOW-COOKER CASSOULET

SAVORY FALL STEW

COCONUT RICE PUDDING WITH BLACK CARDAMOM

WARM PEAR SALAD

Serves 4

Ingredients

★ 2 Bartlett pears, ripe but firm
★ 5 teaspoons olive oil
★ 1 teaspoon honey
★ ½ teaspoon dry mustard
★ ½ teaspoon salt
★ To taste, freshly ground black pepper
★ ½ medium red onion, cut in half, thinly sliced into rings
★ 2 heads endive, sliced crosswise into 1-inch pieces
★ 1 bunch watercress, remove tough stems
★ ¼ pound Roquefort cheese, or another good bleu, crumbled
★ 1½ teaspoons red wine vinegar
★ 1 teaspoon Worcestershire sauce, Lea & Perrins®

Directions

1. Cut pears lengthwise in quarters. Peel, core, and cut the quarters into approximately 1-inch chunks and place in a small bowl. Add 2 teaspoons olive oil, honey, mustard, salt, and pepper, and toss well.

2. Place in a medium skillet over medium-high heat. Add onions and cook until translucent. Add the pears next, careful to keep moving the pan so they do not stick. When the pears have a nice brown hue, remove carefully with the onions.

3. Transfer pears, onions, and any juice into a bowl. Add endive, watercress, remaining olive oil, vinegar, and Worcestershire sauce and toss together gently. Add crumbled cheese, toss again lightly. Season to taste with salt and pepper. Serve while warm.

Jane Kaczmarek and Bradley Whitford   153

SLOW-COOKER CASSOULET

Serves 6

Ingredients

★ ½ pound small white beans, such as pea or navy

★ 4 cloves garlic, peeled and crushed

★ 2 carrots, peeled

★ 2 cups cored and chopped tomatoes, juice as well (canned are fine)

★ 3 or 4 sprigs fresh thyme (or ½ teaspoon dried thyme)

★ 2 bay leaves

★ ¼ pound slab bacon

★ 2 duck legs

★ ¾ pound sweet Italian sausage

★ 1 pound boneless pork shoulder, cut in large chunks

★ Chicken, vegetable stock or water, as needed

★ Salt and freshly ground black pepper

★ 1 cup plain bread crumbs, optional

Directions

1. Combine beans, crushed garlic, onion, carrots, tomatoes, thyme, bay leaves and pork shoulder in a slow cooker. Brown sausage and duck legs in a skillet, add to slow cooker. Add stock or water until it covers ingredients by about 2 inches. Cover and cook until beans and meats are tender, 5 hours on high heat, 7 hours or more on low.

2. When done, add salt and pepper to taste and remove bay leaf.

3. Can be served this way, or you can remove cassoulet from slow cooker, and place in a deep casserole dish: cover with bread crumbs and roast at 400 degrees until bread crumbs turn a nice golden brown, about 15 minutes. Serve and enjoy.

SAVORY FALL STEW

Serves 6

Ingredients

★ 2 tablespoons olive oil

★ 12 ounces hot Italian sausage

★ 12 cipolline onions (pearl onions can be substituted) peeled

★ 1½ cups crushed tomatoes

★ 3 cups homemade or low-sodium chicken stock

★ 1½ ounce bundle of herbs, such as rosemary, thyme, oregano, parsley and 1 bay leaf—tied in a cheesecloth

★ ½ butternut squash, peeled, seeded, then cut into chunks

★ 3 carrots, peeled and cut into chunks

★ 3 parsnips, peeled and cut into chunks

★ 2 celery stalks cut into ¼-inch long pieces

★ 1 fennel bulb, trimmed and cut into ¼-inch-thick slices

★ 12 Brussels sprouts, trimmed and cut in half

★ 2 teaspoons salt

★ ⅛ teaspoon freshly ground pepper

Directions

1. Heat oil in saucepan over medium heat. Remove sausage from casing and crumble into small pieces, cook until no longer pink, about 10 minutes. Remove and place on paper towel, set aside.

2. Discard all but 2 tablespoons fat. Raise heat to medium high, add onions: cook, stirring, 5 to 6 minutes, until golden. Lower heat, add carrots, celery, parsnips, and fennel: cover and simmer until vegetables are tender, about 10 minutes. Add brussel sprouts: cook, covered, about 5 minutes more.

3. Add tomatoes, stock, sausage and herbs: simmer over medium heat until liquid starts to thicken, 20 to 25 minutes.

4. Remove cover, and cook, stirring occasionally, until liquid thickens, 10 to 15 minutes more. Adjust seasoning and serve.

COCONUT RICE PUDDING

Serves 6

Ingredients

★ 1 cup cream, whipping
★ 1¼ cups unsweetened coconut milk, well shaken
★ 2 cups milk
★ 3 black cardamom pods
★ 1½ tablespoons grated lemon zest
★ ½ cup sugar
★ ¼ teaspoon kosher salt
★ 2 cups cold cooked rice (preferably medium-grain)
★ ½ teaspoon vanilla extract
★ ½ teaspoon vanilla bean (scraped)
★ Toasted coconut shavings, for sprinkling

Directions

1. Combine the milks, cardamom pods, vanilla bean. and lemon zest in a medium saucepan and bring to a boil over medium heat. Remove from heat, cool for one hour. Remove vanilla bean pod and refrigerate for 4 hours (or overnight).

2. Strain the cardamom mixture into a medium saucepan. Add the sugar, salt and rice, and bring to a boil over medium-low heat. Reduce heat and simmer, stirring frequently until thick and creamy, about 40 minutes. Stir in the vanilla extract and serve warm or chilled. Garnish with coconut shavings.

Esai Morales

At the age of thirteen, Esai Morales ran away from his Brooklyn home to pursue his dream of acting. He was soon accepted by the prestigious High School for the Performing Arts in New York. He made his film debut in *Bad Boys* with Sean Penn, and then had a featured role in the well known film *La Bamba.* Esai spent three seasons playing "Lt. Tony Rodriguez" on the Emmy-winning TV show *NYPD Blue.* Esai has been honored with both Alma and Imagen Awards for his work.

TreePeople

Started by teenagers in 1973, TreePeople's staff and volunteers have gone on to plant over two million trees in the L.A. area. TreePeople revitalizes inner-city communities, brings neighbors together, and offers sustainable solutions to urban ecosystem problems. Best known for planting and caring for trees, TreePeople has one of the nation's largest environmental education programs and also works with government agencies on critical water issues. Using forest-inspired technologies, TreePeople addresses the nation's most urgent urban eco-problems including water and air quality, energy conservation, and flood prevention. Thanks to the generosity of supporters from around the United States, TreePeople continues to help nature heal our cities, setting the standard for sustainability and civic engagement.

"I like to describe myself as an 'actorvist'—I combine art and activism to build bridges between communities. Environmental stewardship has been a passion of mine for many years. I'm a founding board member of ECO (Earth Communications Office). I have worked internationally with the Wildlife Preservation Fund in Costa Rica, and in Southern California I support TreePeople. I first became involved with TreePeople in 2000 when I appeared in a public service announcement for their Generation Earth youth program. I also emceed their Rock the Earth Concert in Long Beach, California in 2001. I like the fact that TreePeople was started by teenagers—president Andy Lipkis started TreePeople when he was fifteen years old. Their programs involve communities throughout Los Angeles, including underserved neighborhoods and youth at risk. TreePeople's hands-on approach blends the science of urban forestry with an understanding of human behavior—basically, they empower people to take personal responsibility for the planet."

—*Esai Morales*

P uerto Ricans, like everyone, love to eat and in so doing have perfected the art of Caribbean cuisine. Puerto Rican cuisine is among the most flavorful in the world, with roots in Spanish, African, and Taino cooking. Below are a few items, some traditional, some not, which I invite you to try! You can have a Caribbean-themed dinner party and request "tropical casual" attire for fun and comfort.

Catch the Caribbean Wave

COQUITO

CUBA LIBRE

CARIBBEAN SPINACH, CRAB, AND HAM SOUP

ARROZ CON GANDULES

SOFRITO

TEMBLEQUE

© 2006 Esai Morales. Used with permission.

COQUITO

"This is our Christmas, New Year, and The Three Kings traditional holiday drink similar to eggnog in Puerto Rico. It's so yummy you forget there's rum in it . . . but watch out!"

Serves 12

Ingredients
- ★ 1 can (13.5 ounces) coconut milk
- ★ 1 can (13.5 ounces) coconut cream
- ★ 1 can (12 ounces) evaporated milk
- ★ 1 bottle (10 ounces) white rum
  (I recommend Bacardi® or Don Q®)
- ★ ½ teaspoon ground cinnamon
- ★ ½ cup of sugar
- ★ 1 tablespoon vanilla extract

Directions

1. Mix the ingredients in a blender and keep refrigerated. Serve well chilled.

CUBA LIBRE

"Puerto Rican Rums are known worldwide as the best because they are aged for years according to law. Enjoy this Rum and Coke (Cuba Libre), which is one of the local favorites."

1 Cocktail

Ingredients
- ★ Ice
- ★ ¼ glass of Puerto Rican rum
- ★ ½ lime
- ★ Coca-Cola®

Directions

1. Fill a glass with ice. Fill cup ¼ of the way up with Puerto Rican rum. Squeeze the lime juice into the glass. Top with Coca-Cola.

CARIBBEAN SPINACH, CRAB, AND HAM SOUP

"Since many Puerto Rican foods are high in carbohydrates,
I wanted to share a dish with you that is somewhat health conscious.
If you're dieting, you can eat this dish and feel satisfied."

Serves 4 to 6

Ingredients

★ 1 tablespoon butter

★ 1 large onion, minced

★ 1 clove garlic, minced

★ 2 cups spinach, finely chopped

★ 3 cups chicken broth

★ ½ cup skim milk

★ ⅛ teaspoon coconut extract

★ ⅛ teaspoon white pepper

★ 4 ounces imitation crabmeat

★ 3 ounces ham, cut into thin strips

★ ⅛ teaspoon hot pepper sauce (optional)

Directions

1. In a large saucepan, melt the butter over medium-low heat. Reduce heat to low and add the onion and garlic. Cook, covered, for 3 to 4 minutes stirring occasionally. Add the spinach and cook, uncovered, for 2 minutes. Add the broth, milk, coconut extract, and white pepper. Reduce heat and simmer, uncovered, for 3 to 4 minutes.

2. Add the crabmeat and ham and, if using, the hot pepper sauce. Cook for 2 to 3 minutes, or until meat is warmed through. Serve warm.

ARROZ con GANDULES

"The main dish in Puerto Rico during the Christmas holidays
is arroz con gandules (rice and pigeon peas). If you are a
vegetarian, leave out the beef stock. I promise that you will have
a wonderful, tasteful experience."

Serves 4 to 6

Ingredients

★ ⅓ cup sofrito (recipe follows)
★ 2 tablespoons vegetable oil
★ 2 cups rice
★ 3 cups water or beef stock
★ 1 can gandules in their liquid
★ 2 tablespoons tomato sauce
★ ½ teaspoon kosher salt

Directions

1. In a large pot over medium heat, simmer the sofrito in the oil for 2 minutes, stirring constantly. Add the remaining ingredients and mix thoroughly.

2. Cook on high heat until the water evaporates and the surface of the rice is exposed, but not completely dry. Immediately lower heat to a simmer and cover.

3. Cook covered, approximately 20 minutes. Remove cover, taking care to not let the water that has condensed on the cover drip back into the pot! Using a large serving spoon, carefully mix the rice by taking scoops from the side furthest from you and gently placing them toward the center of the pot. Then turn the pot ¼ turn. Repeat 3 times.

4. Taste the rice. It should be slightly firm, but not hard. If it's hard, cover and cook another several minutes and test again. If it's soggy (uh-oh!), cook uncovered several minutes, turn again, and test. Repeat if necessary. Serve hot.

SOFRITO

"The seasoning is perhaps the most noticeable difference in Puerto Rican cookery. The real secret of authentic Puerto Rican flavoring lies in the use of sofrito, a combination of ingredients used as a seasoning to give a distinctive, characteristic taste to many native dishes."

Makes 1 cup

Ingredients

★ 1 large bell pepper, halved and seeded
★ ½ bunch of cilantro leaves
★ 4 stems Recao, or substitute cilantro stems
★ 1 large onion
★ 3 garlic cloves
★ 1 teaspoon dried oregano
★ 5 ajíes dulces, or substitute other mild chile pepper

Directions

1. Place all the ingredients into a blender and purée. Use immediately, or store refrigerated in an airtight glass container for later use. You can also freeze in ice cube trays and store the frozen cubes in a freezer bag.

TEMBLEQUE

"This is one of the recipes that reminds me of my childhood. This pudding is a very common Puerto Rican dessert. It is a creamy coconut pudding, topped with cinnamon, and it is delicious."

Serves 4

Ingredients

★ 1 can (13.5 ounces) coconut milk
★ ½ cup sugar
★ ½ cup cornstarch
★ ¼ teaspoon kosher salt
★ 1 teaspoon vanilla extract

Directions

1. Blend all ingredients, except the vanilla extract, thoroughly.

2. Cook in a saucepan over medium heat, stirring continuously, until it thickens. Add the vanilla, stir, and remove from heat.

3. Pour into individual dessert cups or a shallow dish. Cover and refrigerate for several hours or overnight. If desired, sprinkle with ground cinnamon or ground nutmeg when serving.

Esai Morales 169

Wolfgang Puck

olfgang Puck has changed the way Americans cook and eat by mixing formal French techniques and Asian- and California-influenced esthetics with the highest-quality ingredients. He has also changed the face of dining in cities throughout the nation, beginning in Los Angeles. More recently, he was the first star chef to create a contemporary fine dining restaurant in Las Vegas, thereby leading the way for other celebrated chefs and the city's metamorphosis into a food haven. The Austrian-born Puck began his formal training at age fourteen, inspired by his mother, Maria, a hotel chef. Encouraged by a friend, Wolfgang—whose first name alone identifies him across America—left Europe in 1973 at the age of twenty-four, having already learned his craft as a classically trained French chef in master kitchens. Puck made the move to Los Angeles in 1975 and became both chef and part owner of Ma Maison, which quickly became a magnet for the rich and famous, with Puck the starring attraction. Spago followed in 1982 and so did his first signature dishes—such as "gourmet" pizzas.

WILD RICE AND ARBORIO RISOTTO
WITH SAUTÉED APPLE

"One of my favorite ways to cook and eat wild rice is as part of a risotto, the Italian rice dish featuring short, plump grains such as Arborio, Carnaroli, or Vialone Nano, all of which have generous surface starch that dissolves during cooking to give risotto the creamy sauce that surrounds each pleasantly chewy grain. By combining precooked wild rice with the mixture, you add yet another flavor, texture, color, and shape that wonderfully complement those of the white rice.

When you shop for wild rice, look for it packaged in clear plastic that lets you check to make sure the grains are clean and largely unbroken. Once you open the bag, store in an airtight container in the pantry.

Prepare wild rice separately from other grains, because it requires more water than common rice and takes longer to cook. Generally, you'll need up to three times as much liquid as the volume of wild rice you're cooking. Simmer the grains gently, covered, for about three-quarters of an hour, until they appear to have burst open and are tender but still chewy. Then, drain off any excess liquid by pouring the wild rice into a strainer. In the recipe that follows, you can add any liquid you pour off to the stock you use for the risotto.

You can cook the wild rice and the sautéed apple long before you make the risotto, and reheat gently before adding to the risotto. I like the risotto to be liquid enough so that if you tip the plate, it slides over the plate into a large flat layer."

—*Wolfgang Puck*

WILD RICE AND ARBORIO RISOTTO
WITH SAUTÉED APPLE

recipe courtesy Wolfgang Puck, *Wolfgang Puck Makes it Easy,* Rutledge Hill Press, 2004. All rights reserved.

Serves 4 to 6

Ingredients

For the wild rice
★ 1 cup wild rice
★ 2 tablespoons unsalted butter
★ 1 shallot, minced
★ 3 garlic cloves, minced
★ 3 cups chicken or vegetable stock
  or broth, heated
★ ¾ teaspoon kosher salt
  (less if the stock is salted)
★ Freshly ground black pepper

For the sautéed cinnamon apple:
★ 2 tablespoons unsalted butter
★ 1 apple, peeled, cored, and
  cut into ¼ inch dice
★ 2 tablespoons sugar
★ 1 3-inch cinnamon stick
★ Kosher salt and freshly ground
  black pepper

For the risotto:
★ 3 cups chicken or
  vegetable stock or broth
★ 2 tablespoons unsalted butter
★ 2 tablespoons extra virgin olive oil
★ 1 shallot, minced
★ ⅔ cup Arborio or Carnaroli rice
★ ⅓ cup dry white wine
★ Kosher salt and freshly ground
  black pepper
★ ¼ cup freshly grated
  parmesan cheese

Directions

1. Prepare the wild rice. Put the rice in a fine-mesh sieve, rinse under cold running water, and drain. In a heavy saucepan over medium heat, melt the butter. Add the shallot and sauté until translucent, 3 to 4 minutes. Add the garlic and sauté for another 30 seconds, until fragrant. Add the wild rice and stir to coat it evenly with the butter. Pour in 2½ cups of the hot stock or broth, add salt and pepper, and bring to a boil. Reduce the heat to maintain a bare simmer, cover the pan, and cook until the wild rice is tender but still chewy, 45 to 50 minutes, stirring occasionally and adding more stock as necessary if the liquid in the pan is absorbed before the rice is done. Drain off any stock remaining in the pot and add it to the stock you will use for the risotto. Fluff the rice with a fork, cover the pan, and set aside. Keep warm.

2. Make the sautéed cinnamon apple. Melt the butter in a small sauté pan over medium heat. Add the diced apple, the sugar, and the cinnamon stick and sauté until the apple is glossy and tender, 3 to 5 minutes. Season lightly to taste with salt and pepper. Remove the cinnamon stick. Cover and set aside.

3. Make the risotto. In a saucepan, bring the stock or broth to a boil and reduce the heat to keep it barely simmering. Heat the butter and olive oil together over medium heat in a large heavy skillet or saucepan, add the shallot, and sauté until translucent, 3 to 4 minutes. Add the Arborio rice and stir to coat it evenly with the butter. Stir in the wine and simmer until the pan is almost dry, 2 to 3 minutes. Using a ladle, add 1 ladleful of simmering stock or broth to the rice. Cook the rice, stirring continuously with a wooden spoon, until the liquid has been almost completely absorbed. Add another ladleful and repeat the process until you have used up most or all of the liquid and the rice is tender but still chewy and surrounded by a creamy and slightly runny sauce, 20 to 25 minutes. Taste and add salt and pepper as desired. Stir in the reserved cooked wild rice.

4. If necessary, reheat the apples gently. Stir half of them into the risotto mixture. Taste and adjust the seasonings. Spoon the risotto mixture onto warm plates, sprinkle on the parmesan, top with the remaining apples, and serve immediately.

Wolfgang Puck

Don Most

D on Most is best known for his role as "Ralph Malph" on the classic sitcom *Happy Days.* He continues to guest star in both TV and film, with recent appearances in *EDTV, Century City, Family Guy,* and *Sabrina, the Teenage Witch.* Currently, he has added directing to his repertoire with two independent feature films, *The Last Best Sunday* and *Searching for Mickey Fish.* Don enjoys the game of golf and has played in celebrity tournaments all over the country to benefit various charities.

City of Hope is an innovative research and educational institution dedicated to the prevention and cure of cancer and other life-threatening illnesses. City of Hope is based in Southern California but has had significant worldwide effects on research and treatment for more than fifty years. It is a world leader in developing new treatments for cancer for adults and children, including transplants. It is renowned for its scientific contributions and the way they treat patients with cancer. Some of the most significant advancements include two of the leading anticancer drugs, which evolved because of research pioneered by City of Hope scientists. Also, millions of diabetics benefit from synthetic insulin, which was also developed through City of Hope. City of Hope believes in the power of world-class research and its impact on people all over the globe.

"I initially became aware of the City of Hope over 25 years ago, when my parents became involved in the organization. They had several friends who had been helped greatly by the efforts of their excellent facilities, doctors, caring staff, and administrators. I then became increasingly aware of all the great work City of Hope does for cancer victims and their families. The City of Hope continues to dedicate itself to fighting this terrible disease."

—Don Most

Every few years we like to give a party during the Holiday season. Since we have many friends and family who observe both Hanukkah and Christmas, we came up with the idea of a party theme that would cover both. Hence our "Deck the Halls, with Matzo Balls" Party. These wonderful recipes were handed down through family and friends. We fill the buffet table with many different dishes, so everyone can enjoy a taste of both holiday foods.

*Our Deck the Halls
with Matzo Balls Celebration*

BLITZEN BELLINI

CHRISTMAS PASTA SALAD

AUNT CYNTHIA'S NOODLE KUGEL

JOYCE'S POT ROAST

SANTA'S FAVORITE CRANBERRY MUFFINS

BUBBIE'S BLONDE BROWNIES

BLITZEN BELLINI

Ingredients

★ 1 oz. peach schnapps
★ 2 oz. rum
★ 1 oz. peach nectar

Directions

1. Put in blender with ½ cup crushed ice.

2. Blend, then add ¾ cup champagne: blend, alternating with more crushed ice.

3. Pour into champagne flutes.

CHRISTMAS PASTA SALAD

"The ingredients are red and green."

Ingredients

★ 2 boneless, skinless chicken cutlets (1 whole breast)

★ Paul Prudhomme's Seafood Magic® seasoning

★ 1 package (1 pound) rotini pasta

★ 1 red bell pepper, diced

★ 1 tomato, seeded and diced

★ ½ red onion, diced

★ 1 bunch basil, chopped

★ Italian dressing

★ Kosher salt and freshly ground black pepper

Directions

1. Preheat oven to 400°F.

2. Wash and pat dry chicken breasts, then season each side generously with Paul Prudhomme's Seafood Magic (yes, it's chicken, but use the Seafood Magic). Place in a pan and bake until done, approximately 30 minutes. Let cool and slice.

3. While the chicken is cooling, cook rotini in a large pot of boiling, salted water. Drain, but do not rinse, and place in a large bowl. Add vegetables, chicken, and Italian dressing of your choice and toss. Season with salt and pepper, and refrigerate for a few hours before serving, so the flavors meld and intensify.

AUNT CYNTHIA'S NOODLE KUGEL
Serves 8 to 10

Ingredients

★ 1 package (1 pound) wide noodles
★ 2 tablespoons kosher salt
★ 6 eggs, beaten
★ 1 pint sour cream, or substitute
  lowfat sour cream
★ 1 teaspoon vanilla extract
★ ¼ cup butter
★ 3 green apples, peeled and sliced thin
★ ⅔ cup sugar
★ ½ teaspoon ground cinnamon
★ ½ cup golden raisins
★ Nonstick spray

Directions

1. Preheat oven to 325°F.

2. Bring a large pot of cold water to a boil, season with 2 tablespoons salt, and cook noodles according to package instructions. Drain and return to warm pot with butter. Add remaining ingredients and mix.

3. Spray a baking dish with nonstick spray and spread noodle mixture into pan evenly.

4. Place pan into a larger pan filled with ½ inch of water, creating a water bath. Cook for 45 minutes.

JOYCE'S POT ROAST

Serves 6 to 8

Ingredients

★ 1 piece (4 pounds) top round, chuck, or rump roast, tied if necessary

★ Kosher salt and freshly ground black pepper

★ ¼ cup flour for dredging

★ 2 tablespoons canola oil

★ 8 cipollini onions or 1 chopped onion

★ 1 large clove garlic

★ 1 cup beef stock

★ 12 baby carrots

★ 12 baby new potatoes

★ ½ cup ketchup

Directions

1. Season meat with salt and pepper and dredge in flour. Heat the oil over medium-high heat in a Dutch oven or other heavy pot that can later be covered; brown meat on all sides. Add onions, garlic, beef stock, and ketchup. Cover and simmer for 2 hours on stove, turning meat once or twice.

2. Preheat oven to 325°F.

3. Add potatoes and carrots, replace cover, and place pot in the oven for another hour. Remove when potatoes and carrots are tender.

4. Remove meat from pot and cover with foil to keep warm. Skim the fat from the surface of the remaining juice. Heat the pot and reduce the liquid by half. To serve, slice the meat and serve it with the pan juice.

SANTA'S FAVORITE CRANBERRY MUFFINS

Serves 12

Ingredients

★ ½ cup butter, softened

★ ½ cup sugar

★ ½ cup brown sugar

★ ¾ tsp vanilla

★ ¼ cup milk

★ 1 cup mashed banana

★ 2¼ cups all-purpose flour

★ 1½ teaspoons baking powder

★ ¾ teaspoon baking soda

★ ¾ teaspoon ground cinnamon

★ 1¾–2 cups cranberries
  (if you like tart, use 2 cups)

Directions

1. Preheat oven to 325°F.

2. Cream butter with sugars until fluffy. Add vanilla, milk, and mashed banana.

3. In a separate bowl, combine dry ingredients and stir into banana mixture until just incorporated. Do not overmix. Add the cranberries.

4. Scoop batter into a muffin tin lined with paper muffin liners. Bake for 20 to 30 minutes, until a toothpick or cake tester inserted into a muffin comes out clean (unless you hit a cranberry!). Serve warm.

BUBBIE'S BLONDE BROWNIES

Serves 12

Ingredients
★ 1 cube butter, melted
★ 2 cups brown sugar, packed
★ 2 cups flour
★ 2 eggs, beaten
★ 2 teaspoons baking powder
★ ½ teaspoon salt
★ 1 teaspoon vanilla
★ 1 cup walnuts (optional)

Directions

1. After melting butter in a saucepan, pour into large bowl and add the rest of the ingredients. Mix well, then pour batter into a greased and floured pan.

2. Bake at 350°F for 20 minutes or until toothpick inserted into center comes out clean.

Bob Saget

Bob Saget is a family guy, as evidenced not only by being a father to three daughters, but also by his long run as "Danny Tanner" on the hit sitcom *Full House* and his host duties on the equally successful television show *America's Funniest Home Videos.* Lately, his career has taken an edgier direction—as he often parodies his wholesome image in guest roles and in his stand-up act. His sister Gay died of scleroderma and was the inspiration for a TV movie called *For Hope,* which he made about her struggle with the disease.

Scleroderma is a complex and surprisingly widespread illness, affecting as many people as more commonly recognized diseases such as multiple sclerosis and muscular dystrophy. Scleroderma is typically described as a rheumatic disease of the connective tissues. It is a life-threatening illness that is taking the lives of too many friends and loved ones. When the Scleroderma Research Foundation was established in 1987, very few people were aware of the disease. Today, almost two decades later, scleroderma is still not a household name, but through the efforts of the SRF's research program, scleroderma is growing in awareness. After all, the disease affects as many as 300,000 Americans. The SRF will continue to increase global awareness and raise the critical funds necessary to win the battle against scleroderma.

"I am very appreciative that a portion of the proceeds from this book will benefit the Scleroderma Research Foundation, a foundation on whose board I serve, which exists solely to find a cure for scleroderma, an often life-threatening, and prevalent illness that took the life of my sister Gay over ten years ago. Her son, my wonderful nephew Adam, also thanks the fine ladies who have put this cookbook together to help so many charities close to so many of our hearts."

—*Bob Saget*

All right, so this may be specific—not something you can make weekly—but I can't help myself, because, other than easy-to-do kabobs (no pun intended) or chicken or fish on the grill, this is one of the few meals I cook a year that I truly believe I do decently. Yeah, whatever, right?

Thanksgiving has become a fun tradition. Though I sometimes cook for large groups—my three daughters, their friends, my parents, my nephew, and my friends—Thanksgiving dinner is one that has set a precedent as something I haven't yet screwed up.

Three Thanksgivings ago, I had the pleasure of having my friend Rodney Dangerfield and his wife, Joan, join my family and friends for an eighteen-person dinner. All Rodney had talked about days before was "the turkey leg." That's all he wanted. So it was obvious I had some pressure. Cooking a turkey just right is no small matter, so I searched the Web, talked to my daughters about what they liked, searched the Web some more, went on Food.com . . . and then found a bunch of recipes I retrofitted into what I thought would make a good meal. I had lots of "just decent" red and white wine to pour into the food as required by the recipes, and was thrilled that no "twelve-steppers" were at this particular meal, so I could make a lot in one pot and not have to section off the booze-laden veggies.

Extras . . .

Salad's a nice starter. I don't go the soup route. And I usually put it all out buffet-like. I like spinach salad with miniature tomatoes and croutons and a light balsamic. Romaine works too with the "Thanksgiving of it all" motif.

I also make a side dish of Brussels sprouts. I sauté some onions in a skillet, add some balsamic vinegar and a little olive oil, throw in a few pounds of fresh Brussels sprouts, each cut in half, and sauté it all until it's got dark brown, slight caramelization goin' on. You can also add some red wine to taste. It's nice to have some extra veggies since the whole meal is about starch.

Sweet potatoes—just cook 'em if you like 'em. I cut 'em in thirds, season with some cinnamon and a little sugar sprinkled on 'em, and bake 'em in the oven on cookie sheets. When a fork sticks in easy and comes out, they're done. And they stay hot for hours. I use them to keep the kids warm when the fireplaces burn out. Just keep 'em on the nightstands.

I wouldn't have rolls, because the meal is already bread squared, but if you want them, some nice soft biscuits, or anything that's soaks up gravy, will be appreciated. It's a "festival of binding . . ."

Epilogue . . .

That Thanksgiving three years ago, my late friend Rodney Dangerfield had his turkey leg. He devoured it like Henry the Eighth. Then he had stuffing, some salad, and a nice slice of fresh apple pie a friend of mine brought, with a dip of healthy vanilla ice cream. He left the table and retired for a little while with his wife, Joan, in the den. About ten minutes later, my oldest daughter came to me in the dining room and said, "Dad, Rodney's smoking pot in the den." I looked at my parents, still eating across the table, and then said to my sweet daughter, "Okay, well, open the sliding door and don't tell Grandmom . . ."

I will always have the memory of that night and will continue making this Thanksgiving feast, which changes every time I make it 'cause I honestly don't know what the hell I'm doing. I just steal from some good chefs and doctor it all up as my grandmother used to do.

MENU

Turkey Day the Saget Way

CRANBERRIES

PERFECT ROAST TURKEY WITH BEST-EVER GRAVY

MUSHROOM GRAVY

SPECIAL STUFFING

PUMPKIN PIE

CRANBERRIES

"The directions are also on the cranberry packages,
but this helps . . ."

Serves 6

Ingredients
★ 6 cups fresh cranberries
★ Juice and zest of 3 oranges
★ 1 cup port
★ 1 cup sugar, less or more if needed, or to taste
★ 2 teaspoons ground cinnamon
★ 2 tablespoons cornstarch

Directions

1. In a small saucepan combine cranberries, orange juice and zest, port, sugar, and cinnamon. Bring to a boil, reduce heat to simmer and cook until cranberries are tender, stirring occasionally.

2. In a small cup mix cornstarch and 1 tablespoon water. Whisk cornstarch mixture into cranberry sauce and cook, whisking, until sauce thickens. Taste and add more sugar, if necessary.

3. Cook until sauce thickens but some whole cranberries remain.

PERFECT ROAST TURKEY
WITH BEST-EVER GRAVY *(see next page)*

Adapted from *Thanksgiving 101* (Broadway Books, 1999) by Rick Rodgers
Serves 16, with about 7 cups gravy

Ingredients

- ★ 1 (18 pound) fresh turkey, preferably free-range
- ★ 12–14 cups of your favorite stuffing, prepared
- ★ 8 tablespoons (1 stick) unsalted butter, at room temperature
- ★ Salt and freshly ground black pepper
- ★ 3 quarts homemade turkey stock or chicken broth

Directions

1. Position a rack in the lowest position of the oven and preheat to 325°F.

2. Reserve the turkey neck and giblets to use in gravy or stock. Rinse the turkey inside and out with cold water. Pat the turkey skin dry. Turn the turkey on its breast. Loosely fill the neck cavity with stuffing. Using a thin wooden or metal skewer, pin the neck skin to the back. Fold the turkey's wings behind the back or tie to the body with kitchen twine. Loosely fill the large body cavity with stuffing. Place any remaining stuffing in a lightly buttered casserole, cover and refrigerate to bake as a side dish. Place the drumsticks in the hock lock or tie together with kitchen string.

3. Place the turkey, breast side up, on a rack in the roasting pan. Rub all over with the softened butter. (Play some Sade while you're doing this.) Season with salt and pepper. Tightly cover the breast area with aluminum foil. Pour 2 cups of the turkey stock into the bottom of the pan.

4. Roast the turkey, basting all over every 30 minutes with the juices on the bottom of the pan (lift up the foil to reach the breast area), until a meat thermometer inserted into the meaty part of the thigh (but not touching the bone) reads 180°F, and the stuffing is at least 160°F, about 4½ hours. Whenever the drippings evaporate, add stock to moisten them, about 1½ cups at a time. Remove the foil during the last hour to allow the skin to brown.

5. Transfer the turkey to a large serving platter and let it stand for at least 20 minutes before carving. Increase the oven temperature to 350°F. Drizzle ½ cup turkey stock over the stuffing in the casserole, cover, and bake until heated through, about 30 minutes.

6. Carve the turkey and serve the gravy and the stuffing alongside. (Sounds easy, but carving the turkey is not always so easy. The key is that it can't be too hot to cut, or it will fall apart.)

Bob Saget 195

BEST-EVER GRAVY

"I'm gravy crazy, so take your pick."

Ingredients

- ★ ¾ cup fat, rendered from turkey
- ★ Melted butter, if needed
- ★ ¾ cup all-purpose flour
- ★ ⅓ cup bourbon, port, or dry sherry (optional)

Directions

1. Pour the drippings from the roasting pan into a heatproof glass bowl or large measuring cup. Let stand for 5 minutes, then skim off and reserve the clear yellow fat that has risen to the top. Measure ¾ cup fat, adding melted butter if needed. Add enough turkey stock to the skimmed drippings to make 8 cups total.

2. Place the roasting pan on two stove burners over low heat and add the turkey fat. Whisk in the flour, scraping up browned bits on the bottom of the pan, and cook until lightly browned, about 2 minutes. Whisk in the turkey stock and the optional bourbon, port, or sherry. Cook, whisking often, until the gravy has thickened and no trace of raw flour remains, about 5 minutes. Transfer the gravy to a warmed gravy boat.

MUSHROOM GRAVY

Serves 10

Ingredients

- ★ 2 tablespoons butter
- ★ 3 pounds mushrooms, chopped
- ★ 2 white onions, sliced
- ★ 4 cloves garlic, minced
- ★ ¾ cup white wine
- ★ 3 tablespoons flour
- ★ 2 cups vegetable broth

Directions

1. In a large pan, heat the butter and sauté mushrooms, onion, and garlic over medium heat until vegetables are soft, about 8 minutes. Add the white wine and reduce.

2. When vegetables are soft, add about 2 to 3 tablespoons of flour, stir and cook for 2 minutes. Add stock. Stir and heat until thickened.

SPECIAL STUFFING

Serves 10

Ingredients

★ 2 pounds mushrooms, sliced

★ 1 large onion, sliced

★ 1 head celery, sliced

★ 10 cloves garlic, minced

★ 2 tablespoons chopped fresh sage

★ 2 teaspoons chopped fresh thyme

★ Freshly ground black pepper

★ 1 cup white wine

★ 1 pound whole wheat bread, cubed
  (I use three kinds of preservative-free breads—
  sourdough, whole wheat, and multigrain)

★ Vegetable broth

★ 1 egg, beaten

Directions

1. Preheat oven to 350°F.

2. In a large pan, sauté the vegetables in white wine. Add herbs and cook until vegetables are tender. In a large bowl, mix vegetables with bread cubes.

3. Add egg and enough broth to make it all quite moist but not soupy.

4. Bake, covered, for 30 minutes. Uncover and continue baking for 15 minutes. Serve with mushroom gravy.

PUMPKIN PIE

Ingredients

- ★ ¾ cup granulated sugar
- ★ ½ teaspoon salt
- ★ 1 teaspoon ground cinnamon
- ★ ¼ teaspoon ground ginger
- ★ ¼ teaspoon ground cloves
- ★ 1 teaspoon flour
- ★ ½ teaspoon vanilla
- ★ 2 large eggs, beaten gently
- ★ 1 can (15 ounce) pumpkin
- ★ 1 can (12 fluid ounces) evaporated milk
- ★ 1 unbaked pie shell

Directions

1. Mix sugar, salt, cinnamon, ginger, cloves, and flour in small bowl. Beat eggs in large bowl. Add evaporated milk, vanilla, and pumpkin. Then add the sugar-spice mixture.

2. Pour mixture into pie shell.

3. Bake in preheated 425°F oven for 15 minutes. Reduce temperature to 350°F; bake for 40 to 50 minutes or until knife inserted near center comes out clean. Check pie halfway through cooking time. If crust gets too brown, put strips of foil over just the crust for the rest of baking time. Let cool. Serve immediately or refrigerate.

Joachim Splichal

Hailed as "Legendary Chef" by *Bon Appetit* and named both *Bon Appetit*/Food Network "Restaurateur of the Year" and among the nation's Top 50 Culinarians by *Nation's Restaurant News*, Joachim Splichal is widely acknowledged as a major contributing force behind the growth of Los Angeles into one of the world's premier dining capitals. Splichal's culinary approach emphasizes a playful yet perfectionist style and his enthusiasm for California's resources translates into innovative and elegant dishes. Splichal's surprising and artful use of ingredients has earned him an international reputation as one of the bright lights of the American culinary scene. Splichal's cuisine can be sampled at his restaurants throughout Southern California, including the flagship Patina at Walt Disney Concert Hall, Nick & Stef's Steakhouse in downtown Los Angeles, and Pinot Provence in Costa Mesa.

SEARED TUNA TOWER OF AHI
WITH AVOCADO, SOYA ONIONS, AND YUZU GRANITA

Serves 10

Ingredients

★ 10 roma tomatoes, ripe
★ 3½ pounds best quality yellowfin tuna
★ 20 green onions
★ 2 avocados, sliced and tossed in lemon juice
★ Green from 2 green onions, bias sliced thinly

Soya Onions:

★ 4 red onions
★ ½ cup rice wine
★ ½ cup rice vinegar
★ 4 tablespoons sugar
★ 1 teaspoon Korean chile flakes
★ ½ cup soy sauce
★ 2 teaspoonS ginger, finely grated
★ 4 cloves of garlic, finely minced

Ponzu Vinaigrette:

★ 12 tablespoons grape seed oil
★ 4 teaspoons soy sauce
★ 2 teaspoons sesame oil
★ 4 teaspoons rice wine vinegar
★ 1 teaspoon sugar
★ ½ teaspoon Korean chile flakes
★ 4 shallots, finely minced

Yuzu Granita:

★ Yuzu juice
★ Orange juice

Directions

1. Preheat oven to 100°F.

2. *For the Ponzu vinaigrette:* combine all ingredients in a bowl and mix well. Season with salt and pepper and add shallots.

3. *For the Yuzu granita:* combine all ingredients in a bowl and pour into a shallow pan. Freeze, scraping ice crystals with a fork about every hour until consistency of shaved ice.

4. Peel and seed tomatoes, quarter, and fry in olive oil for a minute. Place in a single layer on a baking sheet, and bake until they dry out a little, about 1 hour. Remove from oven and cool.

5. Rub tuna with salt and pepper. Sear in hot oil on all sides. The tuna should be raw in the middle. Allow to cool. Sauté green onions in hot olive oil until tender.

6. *For the Soya onions:* peel red onions and cut into ⅛-inch thick slices. In a small pot, combine red onions with rice wine, vinegar, sugar, chile flakes, soy sauce, ginger, and garlic and bring to a boil. Cook for a minute, stirring constantly; correct seasonings and allow to cool.

7. To serve, slice avocado and divide onto 10 plates. Cut tuna into ⅕-inch slices and place one slice each on top of sliced avocado. Top with half of Soya onions and another slice of tuna. Add a layer of tomato, remaining onions, and finish with another slice of tuna. Garnish with sautéed spring onions and drizzle with Ponzu vinaigrette. Sprinkle with sliced green onions around outside and serve with a scoop of granita.

Joachim Splichal 203

Marlo Thomas

As an actress, author, producer, and social activist, Marlo Thomas continues to be a guiding force in the entertainment industry and public issues arena. She has been a constant presence on television for more than 40 years—from her legendary title role in *That Girl* to her critically acclaimed performance in *Nobody's Child* to her winning portrayal of Jennifer Aniston's mom on *Friends*— along the way earning four Emmys, a Golden Globe, the George Foster Peabody Award, and an induction into the Broadcasting Hall of Fame. She also won the Grammy award in 2006, in the category of Best Spoken Word Album for Children, for her *Thanks & Giving All Year Long* recording. She lives in New York with her husband, Phil Donahue.

St. Jude Children's Research Hospital is unlike any other pediatric treatment and research facility anywhere. Discoveries made here have completely changed how the world treats children with cancer and other catastrophic diseases. St. Jude is home to some of today's most gifted researchers. In fact, doctors across the world send their toughest cases and most vulnerable patients to St. Jude. It is a facility where no one pays for treatment beyond what is covered by insurance, and those without insurance are never asked to pay. St. Jude Children's Research Hospital is America's third-largest health care charity, with a model that keeps the costs down and the funds flowing, so the science never stops.

"In 1962, my father, Danny Thomas, founded St. Jude Children's Research Hospital. He always believed that every child has a birthright to good health care. "If you really want to help kids, Danny," a forwarding-thinking research doctor, Lemuel Diggs, told him at the time, "don't just build another hospital. Don't just try to make kids better—try to find out what makes them sick." Together they created the first research and treatment center under one roof. Forty years later, St. Jude is internationally recognized for its pioneering work in finding cures and saving children with cancer and other catastrophic diseases. And it continues to hold fast to two important promises my father made when he founded the hospital: that St. Jude would freely share its scientific breakthroughs with scientific and medical communities worldwide, and that no child would ever be turned away for a family's inability to pay.

As National Outreach Director of St. Jude, I'm part of the team that raises the millions of dollars every year that it takes to pay for the research and treatment done at St. Jude. Working with my sister Terre and my brother Tony, we are keeping our father's dream alive—that "no child should die in the dawn of life." What an enriching legacy he has left us."

—*Marlo Thomas*

My husband, Phil, and I are pushovers for a good old-fashioned Sunday Brunch. That means the menu has to include a full range of classic brunch items—from pancakes and waffles to French toast, omelets, and eggs Benedict, and plenty of fresh fruits. But a brunch Chez Thomas-Donahue wouldn't be complete without a few special items on the table. Here are two of our favorites: Asparagus Quiche and Baby Arugula Salad with Melon.

MENU

Take a Bite Out of the Big Apple— A Sunday Brunch

THREE COLOR MELON BALLS
WITH CHAMPAGNE AND PEACH PURÉE

ASPARAGUS QUICHE

GLAZED BACON

BABY ARUGULA SALAD WITH MELON

© 2005 by Marlo Thomas. Used with permission.

THREE COLOR MELON BALLS
WITH CHAMPAGNE AND PEACH PURÉE

Serves 8

Ingredients

★ 2 ripe peaches, peeled and pit removed, flesh mashed into purée

★ ½ Israeli galia melon, flesh scooped into balls

★ ½ cantaloupe or honeydew melon, flesh scooped into balls

★ ½ small watermelon, flesh scooped into balls

★ 16 ounces champagne or sparkling wine, chilled

★ 8 sprigs fresh mint

Directions

1. Pour 2 tablespoons peach purée into 8 large wine glasses.
   Divide melon balls among glasses and top each glass with 2 ounces champagne.
   Serve each with a fresh mint sprig.

Marlo Thomas

ASPARAGUS QUICHE

"Very often I will make the quiche with soy milk and Egg Beaters®. The dish is already rich from the cheese, so this is a good way to reduce saturated fat. More important, it's delicious this way, too.
We generally serve it at room temperature, but we'll reheat it if asked."

Serves 8

Ingredients

Crust:
★ 6 ounces chilled butter, cut in pieces
★ 1¾ cups all-purpose flour
★ ¼ cup cornstarch
★ ½ teaspoon kosher salt
★ ⅓ cup very cold water

Directions

1. Preheat oven to 350°F.

2. Mix the flour, cornstarch, and salt together in a bowl or food processor. Add cold butter pieces, and mix until the flour and butter combine to resemble coarse cornmeal. (Do this quickly to keep the butter from getting too warm.) Sprinkle the water over the flour–butter mixture, and toss a few times to blend.

3. Turn the dough out onto a floured board. It will still seem grainy, but it will come together with a few turns on the table. Rest the dough for 30 minutes. Roll out into a fluted 10-inch tart pan. Rest again. Line with weights and prebake for about 20 minutes. Remove from oven and cool. Keep oven on.

Ingredients

Quiche Filling:

★ 1 large bunch asparagus, blanched and sliced into ½-inch pieces
★ 1 medium onion, diced
★ 2 teaspoons minced garlic
★ ¼ cup Boursin cheese, crumbled
★ ¼ cup Chevre cheese, crumbled
★ ½ cup sharp Cheddar, shredded
★ ½ cup raclette or any Swiss cheese, shredded
★ 1 pint of half-and-half or soy milk
★ 5 eggs or equivalent egg substitute (approximately 6 ounces)
★ 1 teaspoon lemon zest
★ 1 tablespoon fresh dill
★ 2 teaspoons kosher salt
★ 1 teaspoon ground black pepper
★ ¼ teaspoon nutmeg

Directions

1. While crust is baking, prepare filling. Sauté onion and garlic in a small skillet over medium-high heat until brown. Cool completely.

2. In a bowl, mix the eggs and milk thoroughly. Season with salt, pepper, and nutmeg.

3. Put the baked shell on a tray. Sprinkle some of the grated cheese over the crust. Spread the asparagus, onion, and garlic mixture evenly over that, and dot with the crumbled cheeses. Top with remaining shredded cheese. Pour the custard filling into the shell. (It's best to fill the shell ¾ full while the oven shelf is pulled out, and then fill the shell to the top after the shelf is all the way in. The tart shell is shallow, and custard that spills behind the crust makes removal a little harder.)

4. Bake for approximately 45 to 55 minutes, or until the center has risen. To test whether it is ready, shake gently. If it jiggles as one mass and it doesn't slosh like uncooked custard, it is finished. Cool to room temperature and serve.

GLAZED BACON

Serves 8

Ingredients
- ★ 1½ pounds thick sliced bacon
- ★ ¾ cup brown sugar

Directions

1. Preheat oven to 400°F.

2. Lay bacon slices on a baking pan and sprinkle with sugar. Bake for 10 minutes, remove tray, drain fat, and return bacon to oven until crispy, about 10 more minutes.

BABY ARUGULA SALAD WITH MELON

Serves 6

Ingredients
- ★ 2 large ripe heirloom tomatoes, sliced into wedges
- ★ ½ cup black olives
- ★ 4 cups baby arugula
- ★ 2 tablespoons balsamic vinegar
- ★ 3 tablespoons extra virgin olive oil
- ★ Fleur de sel
- ★ Freshly ground black pepper
- ★ 1 cantaloupe, seeded, peeled, and sliced into wedges

Directions

1. Lay the tomato slices on a plate and season liberally with salt, pepper, 1 tablespoon olive oil, and 1 teaspoon vinegar.

2. In a bowl, toss the arugula leaves lightly with remaining oil and vinegar, and season with salt and pepper.

3. Divide arugula among 6 plates, top with the tomatoes, then the olives. Place a sweet cold cantaloupe wedge on the side.

Kerry Washington

Recently, Kerry Washington has had a run of roles in popular major motion pictures including *The Last King of Scotland, Little Man, Ray, Fantastic Four,* and *Mr. and Mrs. Smith.* She also has guest-starred on many television one-hour dramas such as *Boston Legal.* She graduated from The Spence School, in New York City, in 1994, a noted training ground for many of today's hottest actors.

stepup
women's network

Step Up Women's Network is a nonprofit, membership organization dedicated to strengthening community resources for women and girls. Through hands-on community service, mentoring, and fundraising for women's health and critical issues, Step Up educates and activates its membership to ensure that women and girls have the tools they need to create a better future. Step Up has many ways for members to "Invest, Involve & Inspire." Whether it is through its diverse community programs, dedication to helping women advance their careers, or supporting women's health issues, each program aims to empower both girls and women with the skills and confidence they need to succeed.

"When I first heard about the Step Up Women's Network and the amazing work they do to strengthen community resources for women and girls, I knew that I wanted to support their spirit and their mission. Because of my years spent working with youth in East Harlem, I have a great deal of respect and gratitude for the work accomplished by Step Up Women's Network. They are an inspiration and a powerful example of how we can and must continue to make a difference in the lives of young people. I am proud to support this organization and all the work that they do to improve the lives of women and girls."

—*Kerry Washington*

These recipes are from my friend Marie Lynnette Rivera. I've known Lynnette for over fifteen years. We met in east Harlem while working together as peer educators and artists/activists around the issues of adolescent health and wellness, reproductive rights, sexual education, and arts advocacy. While continuing to do this important work in New York and all over the world, Lynnette also currently co-owns and manages a restaurant in East Harlem with her mother. The restaurant serves delicious and authentic Puerto Rican food that celebrates and honors the community in which it exists.

As young women, Lynnette and I would work long days out in the "field" doing peer education outreach programs in schools and health clinics. At the end of the day, her mother's home cooking was a comforting "welcome home," reminding us that we were loved and appreciated. This food helped to give us strength to continue the work that we were doing. We hope these recipes bring you as much warmth and love as they bring us.

Save the Last Plate for Me

GUINEITOS EN ESCABECHE

PIONONOS

PERNIL A LA BAJARI

DULCE DE LECHOSA

GUINEITOS en ESCABECHE
PICKLED GREEN BANANAS

Serves 8 to 10

Ingredients

- ★ 2 tablespoons plus 1 teaspoon kosher salt
- ★ 18 green bananas
- ★ 2 cups olive oil
- ★ 1 cup vinegar
- ★ 12 whole black peppercorns
- ★ 2 bay leaves
- ★ 1½ pounds Spanish onions, sliced
- ★ 3 garlic cloves, minced
- ★ ½ cup green olives with pimentos, chopped
- ★ ½ green pepper, seeded and finely chopped
- ★ ½ red pepper, seeded and finely chopped

Directions

1. Bring a large kettle of cold water to a boil and add 2 tablespoons of salt. Add bananas, cover, and boil over low heat for 20 minutes. Drain and cool.

2. *For Escabeche sauce:* in a medium skillet, mix remaining ingredients (including 1 teaspooon of salt) and sauté over medium heat for 5 minutes, making sure the vegetables remain firm. Remove from heat and allow to cool.

3. Cut bananas into 1 inch rounds then add to Escabeche sauce. Marinate for an hour before serving. Can be served chilled or at room temperature.

PIONONOS
STUFFED SWEET PLANTAIN ROLLS

Serves 6

Ingredients

★ 1 pound lean ground beef

★ ½ cup chopped pitted green olives

★ 3 large ripe plantains (amarillos)

★ 4 tablespoons vegetable oil for frying

★ 2 tablespoons sofrito (*see page 164, Esai Morales's recipes*)

★ 2 tablespoons tomato paste

★ Kosher salt and freshly ground black pepper

★ Toothpicks

Directions

1. Peel plantains and slice each lengthwise into 4 strips. Heat 2 tablespoons of oil in a large skillet over medium heat, fry plantains until tender and slightly brown. Remove and drain on paper towel. Set aside to cool. Reserve oil.

2. In a large sauté pan, heat 2 tablespoons of oil. Add ground beef, sofrito, salt, pepper, and olives, and cook over medium-high heat for 10 minutes until mixture is brown, stirring occasionally. Cool slightly.

3. Beat eggs in a bowl and set aside. Shape each plantain strip into a round and hold it together with a toothpick. Fill the plantain rounds with the ground beef filling. Reheat the oil used to fry the plantains. Dip each pionono into the eggs and fry on both sides over medium heat until golden brown. Drain on paper towels and remove toothpicks before serving.

PERNIL A LA BAJARI
PORK SHOULDER ROAST

Serves 8

Ingredients

★ 5 tablespoons olive oil

★ 5 tablespoons vinegar

★ 1 tablespoon sofrito

★ 2 tablespoons whole black peppercorns

★ 12 cloves of garlic

★ 2 tablespoons dried oregano

★ 2 tablespoons sazón (Latin seasoning)

★ 6-8 teaspoons kosher salt (1 teaspoon for each pound of meat)

★ 1 (6 to 8 pound) pork shoulder

Directions

1. In a bowl, mix the oil, vinegar, and sofrito. Set to the side.

2. Crush the black pepper, garlic, oregano, sazón, and salt in a pilón (mortar) until it's the consistency of a thick paste. Add the paste to the oil and vinegar mixture.

3. Wash meat and pat dry. Make 15 to 20 deep incisions all over the meat. Rub the mixture into the meat, making sure to place liberal amounts in the incisions. Place meat in roasting pan fat side up. Set in refrigerator overnight.

4. Remove meat from refrigerator 30 minutes before roasting. Preheat oven to 350°F. Drain excess liquid from pan and pour over meat, insert meat thermometer into center of meat without letting it rest against bone or fat, cover meat with foil, and place in the oven. Cook 35 minutes per pound, until thermometer reads 185°F.

Note: For extra crunchy skin, drain excess liquid from roasting pan and cook an additional 30 minutes at 400°F.

DULCE de LECHOSA
CANDIED PAPAYA

Serves 8

Ingredients

★ 3 pounds papaya, peeled, seeded, and cut lengthwise into 1-inch-thick slices
★ 3 tablespoons baking powder
★ 4 cups sugar
★ 1 cup brown sugar
★ 1 cup water
★ 2 tablespoons vanilla extract
★ 3 cinnamon sticks
★ 1 apple, peeled and finely chopped
★ 1 package of white cheese (Queso Blanco), optional

Directions

1. In a large bowl, mix baking powder with ½ gallon water, add papaya, and allow to soak for 5 minutes. Remove papaya and rinse.

2. In a heavy pot, place papaya, sugar, vanilla extract, cinnamon sticks, and 1 cup of water and cook, uncovered, over medium heat for 1½ hours. Add apple and cook for an additional 10 minutes, until syrup is thick and shiny. Allow to cool and store, refrigerated, in a glass container.

3. Serve in glass goblets with 2 thin slices of "Queso Blanco" white cheese, if desired.

Nick Stellino

Born to a loving and colorful Sicilian family in Palermo, little Nick Stellino spent his childhood enjoying the simple elegance of country Italian cooking. Growing up in Italy—where love and food are irrevocably linked—Chef Stellino quickly learned the passion of cooking. Stellino first came to America to attend college and stayed on to work for seven years as a stockbroker with a Wall Street corporation. In the fall of 1992, while working at La Terrazza restaurant in Los Angeles, Stellino was "discovered" by an agency talent scout and eventually selected as the TV spokesman for Ragu® Tomato Sauces. From that lucky break came nationwide exposure and recognition and eventually a contract for a series on public television, appropriately named *Cucina Amore.*

NEW YORK STEAK
WITH BALSAMIC VINEGAR SAUCE

Serves 4

Ingredients

★ 4 New York steaks, cut 2-inches thick
  (12–14 ounces each)
★ 1 teaspoon salt
★ 1 teaspoon pepper
★ ½ tablespoon onion powder
★ 1 teaspoon paprika
★ 3 tablespoons extra-light olive oil
★ Balsamic Vinegar Sauce (recipe, right)

Directions

1. Preheat oven to 450°F.

2. Preheat a pan big enough to hold your steaks
   and heat over high heat until it is very hot,
   about 3 to 4 minutes. Mix all the dry spices
   together in a small bowl. Pat the steaks dry
   with a paper towel and rub with the olive oil.
   Sprinkle the top of the steaks with half of the
   spice mixture.

3. Place the steaks, seasoned-side down, into the
   preheated pan and cook for 2½ to 3 minutes
   without turning. Sprinkle the uncooked side of
   the steaks with the remaining spice mixture,
   turn the steaks, and cook on the other side for
   2½ to 3 minutes. (When you are cooking for a
   large party, at this stage of the recipe, you can
   place the steaks on a cooling rack to rest, up
   to 40 minutes. When you are ready to serve,
   place the steaks in the preheated oven to finish
   cooking.)

4. Place the steaks (in the same pan) in the oven
   and cook them for 8 to 15 minutes, keeping in
   mind that 8 minutes will yield medium–rare
   and 15 minutes will yield well-done steaks.
   Cook the steaks to your liking and serve them
   with the Balsamic Vinegar Sauce.

Balsamic Vinegar Sauce

★ 2 tablespoons olive oil
★ 1 tablespoon butter
★ 4 garlic cloves, thickly sliced
★ ½ onion, chopped
★ 1 teaspoon red pepper flakes
★ 1 tablespoon chopped fresh rosemary,
  ground into a fine powder or
  1 teaspoon dry rosemary
★ 2 cups balsamic vinegar
★ 2 cups chicken broth
★ 1 tablespoons of softened butter mixed
  with 1 tablespoon of flour into a
  soft paste (optional)

Directions

1. In a saucepan, cook the butter and garlic
   over medium heat for 2 to 3 minutes.
   Add the onion, rosemary, and the red
   pepper flakes and cook for 4 more minutes.
   Add the balsamic vinegar, raise the heat to
   high, and cook stirring well until it reduces
   by half, about 5 minutes. Add the broth,
   bring to a boil then simmer for 35 to 40
   minutes. If you like the sauce thicker bring
   it back to a boil, and add the butter-flour
   paste 1 teaspoon at the time whisking well,
   until it reaches the consistency you like.
   You do not need to use all of the paste.

2. If you like a fancier look strain the sauce
   through a fine mesh and before you serve
   it place back in the sauce pan and over low
   heat, add 1 tablespoon of plain softened
   butter, stirring well until it is all melted.
   This will add some sheen to the sauce.

Treat Williams

Treat Williams has become a fixture on television as "Dr. Andy Brown" on the hit series *Everwood*. His fictitious life in a mountain community is a far cry from his Connecticut roots. He's a prep-school-educated actor whose ancestry goes back to one of the signers of the Declaration of Independence, Robert Treat Payne. Treat has enjoyed a career on both the big screen and the small screen and has played a wide range of characters. He's earned multiple nominations for Golden Globe awards as well as an Emmy Award nomination for his work on the TV movie *The Late Shift*.

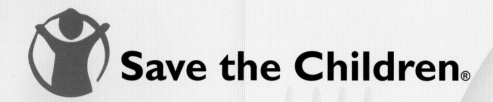

Save the Children®

S ave the Children is the leading independent organization
creating lasting change for children in need in this country
and around the world. The organization works with families
to define and solve the problems their children and communities face,
utilizing a broad array of strategies to ensure self-sufficiency. Through
the decades, the organization has evolved into a leading international
relief and development organization. Domestically, Save the Children
has been working in some of the most impoverished communities in the
country. Today the group focuses its work in twelve states and reaches
thousands of children, providing quality literacy, physical activity, and
nutrition programming. The goal is to create programs that will improve
academic performance, health, and ultimately, children's lives.

"We support Save the Children because children will eventually become the adults who will continue to humanize and improve this beautiful planet. We also did a great deal of research, and found that more than 91% of the money given to Save the Children goes to program services for children and families. Compared to many other charities, this is extraordinary."

—*Treat Williams*

We love Italian cooking because it is so simple and the herbs and spices always complement the pasta, meat, or fish and not the other way around. And garlic and pasta go together so well! The great thing about this menu is that almost everything can be grown in an American garden.

The Heat Is On

SALSA WITH GRILLED FISH

SUMMER PASTA

PAM'S BRUSCHETTA

BLUEBERRY TART

SALSA WITH GRILLED FISH

Ingredients

- ★ ½ clove garlic (diced)
- ★ ¼ red onion
- ★ 3 red vine-ripened tomatoes
- ★ 4 peaches
- ★ 6 fresh mint leaves, chopped
- ★ Dash salt to taste
- ★ Dash pepper to taste
- ★ Juice of 1 fresh lime or lemon
- ★ ¼ teaspoon sugar (if so desired)

Directions

1. Dice equal parts tomatoes and peaches, mix all ingredients together and let sit while you grill the fish. Works well with any fish.

SUMMER PASTA

Ingredients

- ★ 6 tomatoes, seeded and chopped
- ★ 6 zucchinis, thinly sliced
- ★ 1 red onion, chopped
- ★ 1 yellow bell pepper, chopped
- ★ Extra virgin olive oil
- ★ 3 garlic cloves, thinly sliced
- ★ Grated parmesan
- ★ Salt and pepper, to taste
- ★ 1 box spaghetti, cooked al dente

Directions

1. Heat olive oil in a pan until hot.

2. Add onions and peppers until onions are translucent. Add zucchini, season, and cook for about 5 more minutes while watching the heat. Add tomatoes, season, and cook for another 2 minutes.

3. Add garlic, season, and cook until you smell the garlic. Add the al dente pasta.

4. Season again with salt and pepper, place in your favorite pasta bowl, and garnish with plenty of grated parmesan cheese. Enjoy!

PAM'S BRUSCHETTA

Ingredients

- ★ 1 baguette, Italian or French bread
- ★ 3 tomatoes, cut in half and seeded
- ★ 2 cloves garlic, minced plus 1 whole clove for rubbing on sliced bread
- ★ 5 basil leaves, chopped finely
- ★ 1 ounce olive oil
- ★ 1 ounce grated parmesan cheese (optional)
- ★ Salt and pepper, to taste

Directions

1. Slice bread on the bias, and toast in oven or on the grill. After the bread is toasted, rub the cloves of garlic on the bread.

2. Chop the tomatoes into fine, small cubes and place in a mixing bowl. Add minced garlic, balsamic vinegar, basil, salt, and pepper to bowl and let sit for at least 1 hour.

3. Place a spoonful of tomato mixture on top of toasted bread and serve.

BLUEBERRY TART

Serves 6

Ingredients

For crust:

★ 1 frozen graham cracker crust

For filling:

★ 3½ cups blueberries (about 1¼ pounds)

★ ½ cup sugar

★ 3 tablespoons water

★ 2 tablespoons quick-cooking tapioca

★ ½ teaspoon finely grated fresh orange zest

Directions

Make crust:

1. Parbake frozen graham cracker shell until almost done. Take out of oven and let cool.

Make filling:

1. In a 3-quart saucepan combine filling ingredients and bring to a boil, stirring until berries have burst and mixture is liquid. Reduce heat to moderate and cook, stirring occasionally, 10 minutes, or until tapioca is dissolved and filling is slightly thickened. Remove pan from heat and cool filling.

2. Remove rim from tart pan and transfer shell to a plate. Spread filling evenly in graham cracker shell. Let cool in the refrigerator until filling has set. Serve and enjoy.

Alicia Witt

Alicia Witt recently wrapped production on *88 Minutes* opposite Al Pacino for director Jon Avnet. Witt was also seen in *Last Holiday* with Queen Latifah and starred in the critically acclaimed film *The Upside of Anger*. In 2002, Witt appeared in the romantic comedy *Two Weeks Notice* opposite Hugh Grant and Sandra Bullock. Witt combined her acting talents with her skills as a classically trained pianist in the romantic comedy *Playing Mona Lisa*, a role that earned her a Best Actress Award at the US Comedy Arts Festival. On television, Witt has made guest appearances on *The Sopranos* and *Ally McBeal* and previously starred for four seasons as Cybill Shepherd's daughter "Zoey" on the hit sitcom *Cybill*.

The Art Of Elysium

The mission of The Art of Elysium is to encourage working actors, artists, and musicians to voluntarily dedicate their time and talent to children who are battling serious medical conditions. The group provides artistic workshops in the following disciplines: acting, art, comedy, fashion, music, radio, self esteem, songwriting, and writing. The Art of Elysium believes that there is a powerful and mutual exchange of hope and appreciation that occurs when artists share their time and talent with children in poor health. The lives of these children are largely filled with suffering, loneliness, fear, and regimen. An artist has the unique ability to step into their lives and help them find their creative voice, showing the children they have power in the midst of the most difficult circumstances to express their individuality and inner life force. In return, the artists, who have been taken outside of their normal scope of work, have been stretched and enriched in ways they never imagined. Through this inimitable exchange between artist and child, the artist experiences the power of giving and the child experiences the power of their own artistic journey. In fact, "elysium" means a place or condition of ideal happiness.

"I support The Art of Elysium because of the great work of its founder, Jennifer Howell, and her dream of allowing artists and entertainers to bring joy, hope, and laughter to seriously ill children through sharing their gifts and their art with them. It is so important, and especially for those of us who are incredibly lucky to be making a career as artists, to remember that, at this very moment, there are children living close by who have lost even the will to go on. Through The Art of Elysium we can help restore youth and light to these children, and often literally give them the hope they need to survive."

—*Alicia Witt*

My menu has some healthy and sinfully good aspects to it. The salad is an unusual spin on the ordinary baby spinach/sliced pears/caramelized walnuts/dried cranberries salad I usually make. This salad is better for smaller or more elegant groups, since it is served on individual plates rather than brought out in a big family-style bowl to let everyone help themselves. As for the mushroom cakes, I love this recipe because so much of it can be made ahead of time, and once it's complete you have enough little appetizers to bring out before the meal and to keep replenishing them. It's not a quick recipe to make, but if you have time, it's well worth it. They're unique and very delicious. The vinaigrette is especially good, there's always extra, and it can be used on anything.

From the Garden to the Sea

WILD MUSHROOM CAKES

ROASTED TOMATO VINAIGRETTE

HARICOTS VERTS SALAD

HALIBUT "OSSO BUCO"
WITH TOMATO SAFFRON SOY SAUCE

MOCHA CHOCOLATE GENOISE TART

WILD MUSHROOM CAKES

Serves 6

Ingredients

★ 1 large (1½ pounds) eggplant, peeled and cubed
★ 4 teaspoons sea salt, plus additional for seasoning
★ 2 tablespoons extra virgin olive oil, divided
★ 2 tablespoons minced garlic
★ 1 cup chopped onions
★ 2 tablespoons balsamic vinegar
★ 2 tablespoons dry cooking sherry
★ 1 cup sliced cremini mushrooms
★ Freshly ground black pepper
★ ¼ cup chopped fresh basil leaves
★ ¼ cup minced fresh parsley
★ 2 tablespoons parmesan or soy parmesan
★ 2 tablespoons egg whites (from about 1 egg)
★ ½ cup whole wheat bread crumbs
★ 1 recipe Roasted Tomato Vinaigrette (*see next page*)

Directions

1. In a colander, toss the eggplant with the salt. Let sit for 20 to 30 minutes, rinse thoroughly, and pat dry with paper towels.

2. Heat a large nonstick skillet over medium heat and add 1 tablespoon olive oil. Add the garlic and onions and cook, stirring, until the onions are translucent, about 3 minutes. Add the eggplant and cook, stirring, for 5 minutes more. Add the vinegar, sherry, and mushrooms. Continue to cook until the eggplant is softened, 5 to 10 minutes more. Season with salt and pepper to taste. Add the basil and parsley and transfer into a mixing bowl.

3. When mixture has cooled a bit, place it on a cutting board and chop fine. Place the chopped mixture back in the bowl and fold in the parmesan and egg whites.

4. Divide the mixture into 12 equal parts and roll into balls. Roll each ball in the bread crumbs and flatten with spatula slightly to form cakes. Place on a baking tray and refrigerate minimum 2 hours before cooking.

5. Preheat the oven to 350°F. Heat a large nonstick skillet over medium heat and add remaining 1 tablespoon olive oil. Add the cakes and cook until browned 3 to 4 minutes a side. Place on a baking tray and bake for 5 to 7 minutes. Serve with Roasted Tomato Vinaigrette.

Note: For a cocktail party, make 24 small cakes instead of 12 appetizer-size cakes.

Alicia Witt

ROASTED TOMATO VINAIGRETTE

Serves 6

"Although this sauce is perfect to serve with the Wild Mushroom Cakes, it also goes well on grilled fish and chicken—especially in the summer months, when the tomatoes are extra meaty and ripe."

Ingredients
★ 12 ripe plum tomatoes
★ 1 teaspoon minced garlic
★ 1 teaspoon minced shallots
★ 4 tablespoons extra virgin olive oil
★ ½ butternut squash, peeled, and cut into pieces
★ 2 tablespoons Dijon mustard
★ 2 tablespoons sherry vinegar
★ 1 tablespoon chopped fresh basil leaves
★ Kosher salt and freshly ground black pepper

Directions

1. Preheat the oven to 325°F.

2. Slice each tomato into 3 pieces. In a mixing bowl, toss the tomatoes with the garlic, shallots, 1 tablespoon of the olive oil, the squash, and the mustard. Place the mixture in a shallow baking dish and roast for 30 minutes. Let cool for 20 minutes.

3. Transfer the mixture to a food processor and purée. Add the vinegar and basil and mix. Season with salt and pepper to taste. While mixing, slowly drizzle in the remaining 3 tablespoons olive oil to emulsify. Can be refrigerated up to 3 days.

HARICOTS VERTS SALAD

Serves 4

Ingredients

★ 1 pound fresh haricots verts, ends trimmed, or substitute green beans

★ 2 teaspoons kosher salt, plus extra for seasoning

★ 2 tablespoons extra virgin olive oil

★ 1 teaspoon red wine vinegar

★ 1 teaspoon lemon juice, fresh preferably

★ Freshly ground black pepper

★ 1 cup arugula, washed and dried

★ ¼ pound pecorino Toscano cheese, shaved into thin slices

Directions

1. Bring a pot of water to a boil and add the haricots verts and 2 teaspoons of salt. Simmer for 5 or 6 minutes, until tender but still crisp. Put in ice bath to stop cooking.

2. In a small bowl, mix the oil, vinegar, and lemon juice. Add salt and pepper. Toss the arugula with 1 tablespoon of the dressing, and toss the haricots verts with the remaining dressing.

3. Divide the beans among 4 plates and top each one with a few arugula leaves. Serve with shaved cheese on top.

Alicia Witt 247

HALIBUT "OSSO BUCO"
WITH TOMATO SAFFRON SOY SAUCE

"This is a great one because it's super easy, and super flavorful, and you
can just toss all your fish into the oven instead of standing at the stove or
grill, preparing it and trying to keep it warm. It's amazing how creamy
this one comes out, without any butter or cream added. "
Serves 4

Ingredients

★ 4 ripe plum tomatoes
★ Sea salt (can substitute kosher
   salt) and freshly ground
   black pepper
★ 1 whole bulb garlic
★ ½ teaspoon extra virgin olive oil
★ Nonstick cooking spray
★ 4 (8 ounce) halibut steaks
★ 1 pinch saffron threads
★ ½ cup plain soy milk
★ 1 tablespoon soy margarine
   (or butter if you like)
★ 1 teaspoon fresh chives, minced,
   or ½ teaspoon dried chives

Directions

1. Preheat the oven to 275°F.

2. Slice the tomatoes in half lengthwise. Season them
   with salt and pepper. Cut off the top of the garlic bulb
   to expose the cloves. Drizzle it with the olive oil.
   Place garlic in baking dish with the tomatoes. Roast
   for 1 hour. Remove from the oven and raise the oven
   temperature to 350°F.

3. Fifteen minutes before the tomatoes and garlic are
   done, season the halibut with some salt and pepper.
   Spray nonstick skillet with cooking spray. Turn
   stove to medium heat. Sear the halibut on both sides
   (approximately 3 minutes per side). Remove from pan
   and place in baking dish. Let the halibut rest at room
   temperature while finishing the sauce.

4. Squeeze garlic from cloves, and quarter the tomato
   halves. Cook the garlic and tomatoes in a nonstick
   skillet over medium heat for 2 to 3 minutes, stirring
   throughout. Add the soy milk and the saffron.
   Whisk in the margarine (or butter) to finish the sauce.
   Add salt and pepper to taste. With a pimer or hand
   blender puree the sauce. Add the chives. Set aside,
   keeping it warm.

5. Finish cooking the halibut in the oven for 8 to 10
   minutes. Serve sauce with halibut.

MOCHA CHOCOLATE GENOISE TART

"This is just about the most decadent and most professional-dessert-chef thing I've ever made successfully. As you can see, this is not an easy preparation, or rather—its not that difficult, it's just extremely time-consuming. But trust me, you cannot imagine how ridiculously good it is!"

Serves 10

Ingredients
- ★ 1 recipe Chocolate pastry (recipe left, below)
- ★ 7 ounces dark chocolate (about 60% cocoa solids), melted
- ★ 1 large egg white
- ★ 2 teaspoons powdered egg white
- ★ ¼ cup sugar
- ★ ¼ cup ground almonds
- ★ 1 tablespoon all-purpose flour, sifted
- ★ 2 tablespoons coffee extract
- ★ 2 tablespoons coffee liqueur, optional
- ★ ½ cup heavy cream
- ★ 4 tablespoons milk
- ★ 2 tablespoons strong fresh coffee, cooled
- ★ 1 large egg, beaten
- ★ ¼ cup sugar
- ★ fresh raspberries

CHOCOLATE PASTRY

Enough for 1 (10-inch) tart crust

Ingredients
- ★ 1¼ cups all-purpose flour
- ★ ¼ cup cocoa powder
- ★ 1 teaspoon fine sea salt
- ★ 2 tablespoons sugar
- ★ 10 tablespoons cold, unsalted butter
- ★ 1 ounce dark chocolate, melted and cooled
- ★ 2 egg yolks
- ★ 2 tablespoons ice water

Directions

1. Sift the flour, cocoa powder, and salt together.

2 In the bowl of a food processor, combine the sugar and butter together into a coarse meal. Beat in the melted and cooled chocolate and the egg yolk.

3 Add the flour mixture and mix to combine. Add cold water until dough binds together. Shape into a flattened ball, wrap in plastic wrap and let rest in the refrigerator for 30 minutes before rolling out.

Directions

1. Line a baking sheet with parchment. Lay the removable base of a 10-inch tart pan on the parchment and draw around it. Return the base to the tart pan.

2. Roll out the pastry dough on a lightly floured surface and line a tart pan with parchment paper; pinch any cracks together. Don't trim the edge, leave it overhanging. Prick the base with fork, line with foil and baking weights. Chill for 15 to 20 minutes.

3. Preheat the oven to 375°F. Place the tart shell on a baking sheet and bake for 15 minutes. Remove the foil and weights, trim the pastry edge level with the top of the pan and bake for 10 minutes, until crisp. Let cool. Turn the oven setting down to 350°F.

4. Spread ⅓ of the melted chocolate evenly over the pastry. Keep the remaining chocolate at room temperature.

5. Make the sponge layer. Whisk the egg white and powder in a bowl until stiff, then whisk in the sugar until glossy and firm. Using a large spoon, carefully fold in the flour and almonds. Spread the mixture over the circle on the

parchment. Bake for 12 minutes. Leave to stand for 5 minutes, then carefully peel off the paper and cool on a wire rack.

6. Heat the coffee extract and liqueur until hot but not boiling, then let cool.

7. Now for the custard, bring the cream and milk to the boil, then pour in the remaining melted chocolate, stirring until smooth. Cool, and then stir in the coffee. Beat the egg and the sugar together, and then mix with the chocolate cream.

8. When ready to assemble, heat the oven to 325°F. Fit the sponge layer into the pastry bottom and slowly pour over the coffee liqueur syrup. Place the tin on its baking sheet on the middle oven shelf, pulling the shelf out as far as it is safe. Pour in the chocolate custard—it should reach the top. Gently push the oven shelf back and bake for about 40 minutes. The filling will be soft—it firms on cooling.

9. Cool until the filling is like mousse. Unmold the tart on to a large flat plate. Garnish with fresh raspberries and cut and serve at room temperature.

Kelley Wolf

Kelley Limp Wolf came into the nation's attention as a participant on the successful MTV series *Real World*. On *Real World,* which was started in 1992, each year producers pick seven people from different backgrounds to live together in a major city. Kelley married actor Scott Wolf in her hometown of Fayetteville, Arkansas. The pair honeymooned in Africa.

Scott Wolf

After a long run as "Dr. Jake Hartman" on the popular family television show *Everwood,* Scott Wolf is starting a new series called *The Nine* for ABC. He has also appeared as "Bailey Salinger" on another popular TV show *Party of Five.* He got his college degree from George Washington University in something far from his current vocation—finance. In May 2004, he married Kelley Limp.

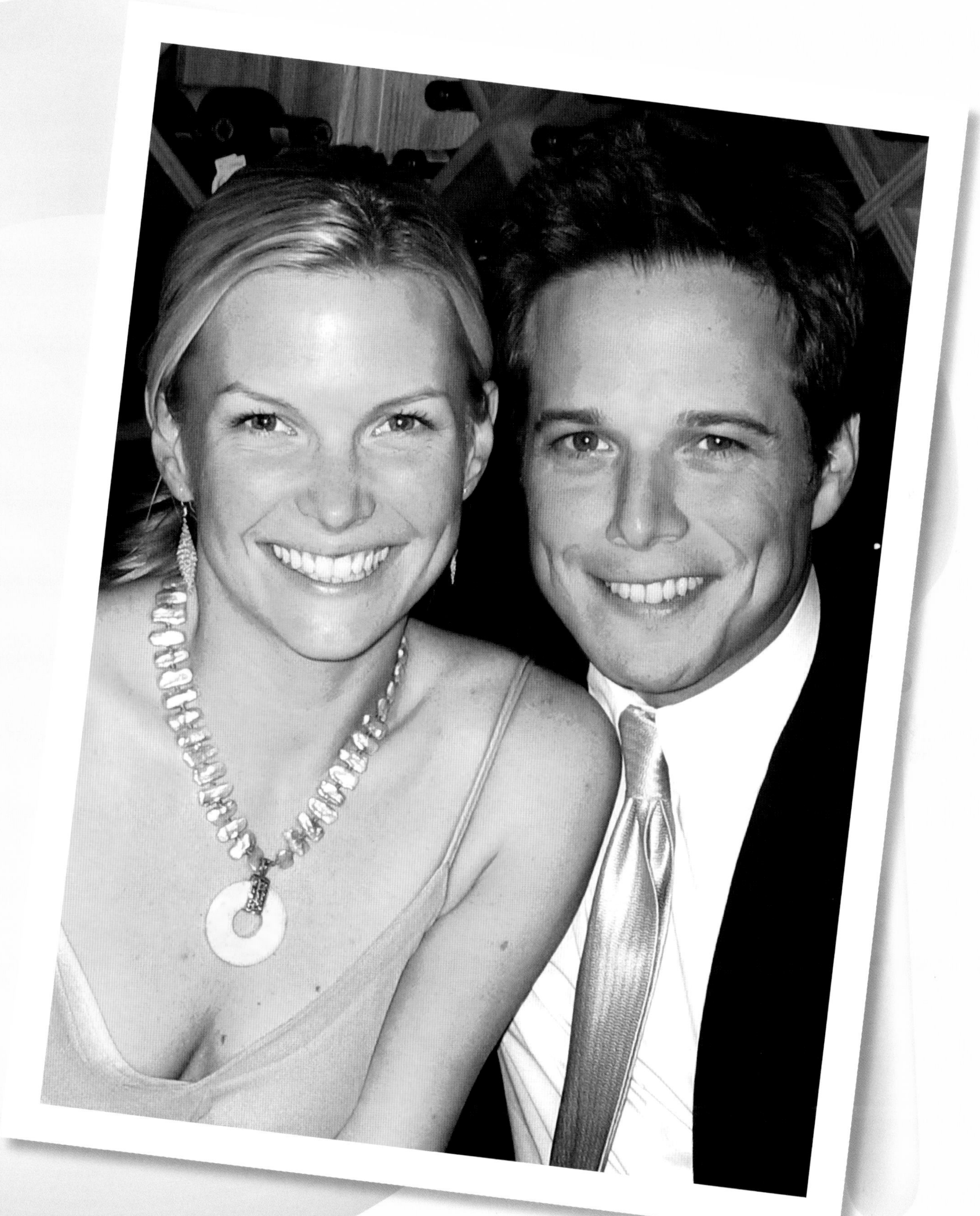

Kelley and Scott Wolf

In 1993, inspired by the struggle of a young boy with AIDS to have a normal life, then twenty-two year-old Neil Willenson founded Camp Heartland—a summer camp program equipped with state-of-the-art medical facilities able to handle the special needs of children with HIV/AIDS. Since that time, Camp Heartland has grown to become a national nonprofit organization where children impacted by HIV/AIDS, as well as those experiencing grief, poverty, and other troubling circumstances, can experience unconditional love and acceptance and increase their self-esteem. What began as Neil's quest to give one little boy a week of friendship and summertime fun, is now a year-round community making a life-long impact for thousands of children and their families. Camp Heartland has expanded both its efforts to impact children globally as well as provide year-round support programs such as camp reunions, newsletters, holiday and birthday gifts, youth retreats, and other life enhancement programs. These services reinforce the young people's sense of belonging and well-being on an ongoing basis.

"We are proud to support Camp Heartland. This incredible group works year round to enrich the lives of children living with HIV/AIDS. From 1993 to the present, the summer camp has provided an amazing experience for kids impacted by HIV/AIDS. We have had the chance to meet many of the children who have been to the camp. The impact the camp has made on their lives is truly special. Campers return to mentor new campers, and they are building a community of friendships that is invaluable."

—*Kelley and Scott Wolf*

The Baked Brie recipe comes from Scott's stepmother, Prudence Wolf. She is known for making food that stops a conversation—your mouth is full, so you can't talk. This is one of the best things we have ever put in our mouths. One warning: share this or you *will* eat it *all* by yourself. As for the Poppyseed Salad, this recipe comes from Scott's sister Jessica. The Wolf house in St. Louis is constantly buzzing with love and family, and this salad is always a favorite. The short ribs recipe comes from my side of the family. My mom made this for Scott a few years ago, and it remains his favorite. This is wonderful on a cold night with a glass of wine and someone you love. Lastly, every Thanksgiving and on some very special occasions, we have this pecan pie. Whenever we look at the recipe, we wonder why we wait until Thanksgiving to enjoy it. It is a simple recipe with great rewards.

Let It Snow— Our Favorite Winter Dinner

NOT YOUR MOTHER'S BAKED BRIE— MY MOTHER'S BAKED BRIE

JESSICA'S POPPYSEED SALAD

BEEF SHORT RIBS with HORSERADISH SAUCE

DAD'S FAVORITE PECAN PIE

NOT YOUR MOTHER'S BAKED BRIE–
MY MOTHER'S BAKED BRIE

Serves 6

Ingredients

★ 1 (8 ounce) brie round

★ ¼ cup brown sugar

★ 4 tablespoons butter, cut into pats

★ ½ cup sliced almonds

★ Crackers to serve

Directions

1. Preheat oven to 400°F.

2. Place brie round in the center of an ovenproof dish and top with brown sugar. Top with pats of butter and then the almonds. Bake for 20 to 25 minutes. Serve hot with crackers.

Kelley and Scott Wolf 257

JESSICA'S POPPYSEED SALAD

Serves 6

Ingredients

★ ¾ cup sugar
★ ⅓ cup cider vinegar
★ 1 cup vegetable oil
★ 1½ tablespoons poppy seeds
★ 1 teaspoon kosher salt
★ 3 cups romaine leaves, chopped
★ 3 cups baby spinach leaves
★ 1 cup sliced mushrooms
★ ½ cup sliced almonds
★ ½ pound bacon, cooked and chopped
★ 1 cup shredded provolone cheese
★ ¼ cup grated parmesan cheese

Directions

1. In a bowl or airtight container, combine sugar, vinegar, oil, poppy seeds, and salt and mix well. Allow dressing to sit for a minimum of 30 minutes before using.

2. In a large salad bowl, mix together remaining ingredients. Toss with dressing and serve immediately.

BEEF SHORT RIBS
WITH HORSERADISH SAUCE

Serves 6

Ingredients

★ 1 cup crème fraiche

★ ½ cup sour cream

★ ⅓ cup prepared white horseradish

★ 6 tablespoons chopped fresh chives

★ 5 tablespoons fresh squeezed
   lemon juice

★ Kosher salt and freshly ground
   black pepper

★ 6 pounds beef short ribs

★ 2 tablespoons olive oil

★ 3 large carrots, peeled, cut
   into ½-inch rounds

★ 2 medium onions, each sliced
   into 8 wedges

★ 1 cup red wine

★ 2 cups water

★ 3 cups beef broth

★ 1 leek, white parts only,
   cut into ¼-inch slices

★ 10 garlic cloves, minced

★ 1 bay leaf

★ 10 sprigs fresh thyme

★ 24 baby red-skinned potatoes

★ 1 medium savoy cabbage,
   cut into 6 wedges

Directions

1. In a bowl, combine first 5 ingredients. Season with salt and pepper and refrigerate.

2. Preheat oven to 350°F.

3. In a Dutch oven, heat olive oil over medium heat. Season ribs with salt and pepper and brown, about 2 minutes a side, in batches if necessary. Remove meat and set on a platter.

4. Add onions and carrots to the pot. Cook for about 3 minutes. Add wine, water, broth, leek, garlic, bay leaf, and thyme. Return ribs to pot and bring to a boil. Cover and cook in the oven for 2 hours. Add potatoes and bake 1 hour longer. The meat should be falling off the bone. Remove and discard bay leaf.

5. Just before serving, steam wedges of cabbage on top of stove until just tender. Divide ribs and cabbage wedges among 6 plates. Top ribs with vegetables, broth, and horseradish sauce. Serve with crusty bread.

DAD'S FAVORITE PECAN PIE

Serves 10

Ingredients

★ 1 prepared frozen pie crust, thawed
★ 6 tablespoons butter, melted
★ 1 cup white corn syrup
★ 1 cup dark brown sugar
★ ⅓ teaspoon kosher salt
★ 1 teaspoon vanilla extract
★ 3 eggs, beaten
★ 2 cups pecan halves
★ Whipping cream
★ Amaretto, optional

Directions

1. Preheat oven to 350°F.

2. In a bowl, mix together butter, corn syrup, brown sugar, salt, vanilla, and eggs. Pour mixture into pie shell. Add pecans and press into pie with a spatula.

3. Bake pie for 40 to 45 minutes, remove from oven and cool. Serve with whipped cream flavored with amaretto.

Charities Participating in
The Hollywood Cookbook

THE ART OF ELYSIUM
100 Universal City Plaza Dr.
Bldg. 6111
Universal City, CA 91608
Phone: 818-773-3449
Fax: 818-866-6612
Web site: www.theartofelysium.org

BOYS & GIRLS CLUBS OF AMERICA
1230 W. Peachtree St. NW
Atlanta, GA 30309
Phone: 404-487-5700
                404-487-5851
Fax: 404-487-5787
Web site: www.bgca.org

CAMP HEARTLAND
3133 Hennepin Ave. South
Minneapolis, MN 55408
Phone: 612-824-6464, ext. 19
Web site: www.campheartland.org

CHILDREN'S LIFESAVING FOUNDATION
31239¼ Bailard Road
Malibu, CA 90265
Fax: (310) 457-4213
E-Mail: info@childrenslifesaving.org
Web site: www.childrenslifesaving.org

CITY OF HOPE
1055 Wilshire Blvd., 12th Floor
Los Angeles, CA 90017
Phone: (213) 241-7201
Web site: www.cityofhope.org

CLOTHES OFF OUR BACK
10 Universal City Plaza, 20th Floor
Universal City, CA 91608
Phone: (818) 753-2404
Fax: (818) 753-2414
Cell: (818) 522-0628
Web site: www.clothesoffourback.org

CRYSTAL PEAKS YOUTH CAMP
19344 Innes Market Rd.
Bend, OR 97701
Phone: 541-330-0123
Web site: www.crystalpeaksyouthranch.org

CURE AUTISM NOW
5455 Wilshire Blvd., Suite 715
Los Angeles, CA 90036
Phone: 323-549-0500, ext. 27
Fax: 323-549-0547
Web site: www.cureautismnow.org

ELIZABETH GLASER PEDIATRIC AIDS
FOUNDATION
2950 31st Street, Suite125
Santa Monica, CA 90405
Phone: 310-314-1459
Fax: 310-314-1469
Web site: www.pedaids.org

HOLLYWOOD HABITAT FOR HUMANITY
17700 S. Figueroa Street
Gardena, CA 90248
Phone: 818-503-2154
Fax: 310-323-0789
Web site: www.hollywoodforhabitat.com
                www.habitatla.org

LOLLIPOP THEATER NETWORK
P.O. Box 455
Old Chelsea Sta.
New York, NY 10113
Phone: 800-545-0814
Web site: www.lollipoptheater.org

MICHAEL J. FOX FOUNDATION
FOR PARKINSON'S RESEARCH
Phone: 212-509-0995, ext. 242
Fax: 212-509-2390
Web site: www.michaeljfox.org

PEDIATRIC EPILEPSY PROJECT
Mattel Children's Hospital at UCLA
David Geffen School of Medicine at UCLA
22-474 MDCC
10833 Le Conte Avenue
Los Angeles, CA 90095-1752
Web site: www.4pep.org

P.S. ARTS
3025 Olympic Blvd., Suite 315
Santa Monica, CA 90404
Phone: 310-586-1017
                310-586-2380
Fax: 310-586-1608
Web site: www.psarts.org

REEL ANGELS
4751 Wilshire Blvd., Third Floor
Los Angeles, CA 90010
Phone: 323-549-4373
Web site: www.reelangels.org

SAVE THE CHILDREN
Corporate Partnerships
54 Wilton Road
Westport, CT 06880
Phone: 203-221-4014
Web site: www.savethechildren.org

SCLERODERMA RESEARCH FOUNDATION
220 Montgomery St., Suite 1411
San Francisco, CA 94104
Phone: 415-834-9444
                 1-800-441-CURE
Fax: 415-834-9177
Web site: www.srfcure.org

STEP UP WOMEN'S NETWORK
3540 Wilshire Blvd., Suite 502
Los Angeles, CA 90010
Phone: 213-382-9164
Fax: 213-559-0595
Web site: www.stepupwomensnetwork.org

ST. JUDE CHILDREN'S RESEARCH HOSPITAL
ALSAC/St. Jude West Hollywood
8282 West Sunset Blvd., Suite B
West Hollywood, CA 90046
Phone: 323-650-9360
Fax: 323-650-9359
Web site: www.stjude.org

TREEPEOPLE
12601 Mulholland Dr.
Beverly Hills, CA 90210
Phone: 818-753-4600
Fax: 818-753-4635
Web site: www.treepeople.org

EIF ENTERTAINMENT
INDUSTRY FOUNDATION™

We are lucky enough to have the ENTERTAINMENT INDUSTRY FOUNDATION (EIF) managing our donor fund. The Hollywood Cookbook Charities Fund will see that the designated proceeds from cookbook sales are directed to the participating charities. Chief Financial Officer Merrily Newton has personally become involved to make sure that this fund works properly. She will supervisor the distribution of funds to the twenty charities involved. EIF is the major intersection of the Hollywood entertainment industry with philanthrophy, taking on initiatives benefiting areas such as childhood hunger, cancer research, creative arts, education, cardiovascular research, and much more. Annually, the Entertainment Industry Foundation funds more than 300 charitable organizations within the greater Los Angeles area and throughout the nation.

MAURICE LACROIX

Switzerland

Tomorrow's Classics

WE GRATEFULLY ACKNOWLEDGE MAURICE LACROIX SWISS WATCHES AS OUR SPONSOR

MAURICE LACROIX SWISS WATCHES provided the seed money that launched this project. Quite simply, without their help, the cookbook would have never materialized. The executives at Maurice Lacroix Swiss Watches believed in this concept from its earliest inception and were always there with encouragement, great ideas, and the funds to make things happen. We'd like to say a special thank you to Maurice Lacroix for stepping up to support these worthwhile causes and truly becoming a partner in this endeavor.

Thank you!

KITCHENACADEMY™

We are delighted to recognize KITCHEN ACADEMY's wonderful contribution to this cookbook. Chefs at this professional culinary school reviewed each and every recipe and tested them for accuracy, taste, and presentation. At times, these talented chefs would make a suggestion for a slight improvement or a bit easier preparation technique, but on the whole, they were delighted with the recipes just as the celebrities sent them in to us. In fact, one instructor told us that the menus exceeded his expectations by a lot. Not only did Kitchen Academy undertake the major task of testing: their skilled students also helped us prepare the recipes for photography in the on-site kitchens on three separate days. As each dish was prepared, a new culinary star was born, and there was definitely a feeling of palpable pride in what was being presented. We thank Kitchen Academy for support, before, during, and after the process of putting together this cookbook—the pros always make it look easy!

Kitchen Academy Staff:
Matthew Bernsen, Instructor
Colette DeShay, Instructor

Students:
Jessica Alfaro
Monica Armstrong
Willard Barna
Floridalma Noemi Benavente
Robert Byazrov
Jeremy D. Castro
Victoria Clark
Lindsay Crolius
Kenneth W. Fryer

Vivian Gonzales
Chastise Hardaway
Tiki Hardaway
Armand G. Helaire
Edwin Henriquez
Arturo Herrera
Nick Kang
Aram Kazaryan
Michael Kesler
Shikaya Lately
Vlad Mamin
Bridget Marroquin
Paul McMaster
Ernest Miller

Aja Mohammed
Leda Mora
Kay Nia
William Ottley
Jocelyne Palant
Sophia Ramirez
Dan Schamrowski
Robert Sheafer
Alan Casey Smith
Gustavo Leon Valadez
Eduardo Velazquez
Mare Wachs
Natalie Walker
April Ward

6370 W. Sunset Blvd. • Hollywood, CA 90028 • www.KitchenAcademy.com

Thank You

Jeff Androsky	Jaime Gwen	Madison Most
Jessica Angel	Brian Hern	Heather Myrick
Holly Barkhymer	Joanne Horowitz	Alan Neirob
David Beckwith	Jennifer Howell	Debra Newman
Jenni Benzaquen	Amy Hudson	Merrily Newton
Wallis Beth	Michael Huey	Sid Pazoff
Carol Birch	Peter Ingram	Susan Pekich
Jane Birnbaum	Evelyn Iocolano	Jennifer Posner
Jeff Black	Rene Jones	Loyda Ramos
Maggie Boone	Ara Keoshkerian	David Ransil
Michael Breitner	Jennifer King	Dr. Melinda Reynard
Danielle Carrig	Matthew King	Raina Ring
Lara Casse	Caryn Leeds	Karen Schneider
Rosser Cole	Danielle Lemmon	Michel Schneider
Julie Condra	Carol Levey	Lynne Segall
Maria D'Angelo	Pamela Lewy	Paul Shane
Mark Davis	Ann Limongello	Amy Shapiro
Stephen Davis	Susan Madore	Carol Sherman
Meghan de Andrade	Hillary Manning	Lisa Shotland
Amy DeBower	Mike Mansel	Amanda Smith
Tara Dhar	Melanie Marconi	Charles Spaulding
Tom Ehrhardt	Stephen Marks	Louisa Velis
Vicki Forman	Francesca McCaffery	Sherry Vrooman
Laura Fox	Danny McGuire	Dr. Sarah Weiner
Patricia Ganguzza	Dana McNaugthton	Anson Williams
Karen Ray Goldberg	Kim Meeder	Jordan Yospe
Joel Goldman	Troy Meeder	Jared Zabel
Greg Grudt	Neil Meyer	Jonathan Zabel
Alexx Guevara	Angela Moore	Lauren Zabel
Danielle Guttman	Mackenzie Most	Lynne Zuckerman

About the Authors

Jackie Zabel

Jackie Zabel is an accomplished Hollywood screenwriter and a one-time member of ATAS Cares, a committee that helped benefit disadvantaged working women and was supported by the Academy of Television Arts and Sciences foundation.

Together with her husband Bryce, a former Chairman of the Academy of Television Arts and Sciences, she is a principal in Stellar Productions, a company focusing on TV and film projects, the latest being *Pandemic,* a medical thriller, on which she shares writing credit.

In 2001, Jackie shared story credit on the Disney summer release *Atlantis: The Lost Empire.* She's also written television episodes and Movies of the Week, and she has optioned both television and feature material to Nickelodeon, Warner Brothers, and Universal. Her career started in local news, writing and producing for KCBS-TV.

Jackie graduated with a Master's degree in Broadcast Journalism from USC. She also earned two undergraduate degrees in Journalism and Psychology from the University of Texas. She graduated Phi Beta Kappa and is the mother of three children.

Morgan Most

Growing up in Los Angeles, Morgan decided early to pursue a career in acting. She almost immediately started landing roles in numerous television drama and sitcoms such as *Vegas, When the Whistle Blows, Dallas,* and *Simon and Simon.*

It was during one of her guest appearances on the TV show, *Happy Days,* that Morgan met actor Donny Most. Two years later, they were married.

Morgan continued to work as an actress, appearing in such projects as the TV miniseries, *My Wicked, Wicked Ways* (the story of Errol Flynn), and the feature film *The Man Who Wasn't There,* co-starring with Jeffrey Tambor and William Forsythe.

When the Mosts decided to start a family, Morgan opted to devote herself full-time to her children, volunteering at their schools, sports teams, and extracurricular activities. Coming from a family dedicated to public service, she has always been involved in community causes, supporting many local charities. Morgan graduated from UCLA with a degree in Theatre Arts.

Contributors

CRAIG T. MATHEW (Photographer), a Los Angeles based photographer has been capturing the Hollywood scene for the past twenty years. An alumni of the prestigious Brooks Institute of Photography, Craig worked for the Associated Press and Los Angeles Times covering world events before starting his own company in 1988. Since 1988, Craig has been the official photographer of The Academy of Television Arts & Sciences. Among his many clients are the well-known Dr. Phil McGraw and Ellen DeGeneres. Other clients are The California State Lottery, Six Flags, Paramount Studios, E! Entertainment, and Sony Studios. He is actively involved in the development of FilmMagic.com, a top-three supplier of entertainment-related photos to the media. In his spare time he volunteers with youth sports and spends time with his family which includes five kids.

ZIVA SANTOP (Photographer) immigrated to the USA from South Africa in 1985. She ran a successful wholesale pastry and catering company. In 2000 Ziva transitioned from a pastry chef to a photographer. She is currently a Public Relations photographer in Los Angeles. Ziva regularly travels to third world countries to photograph the diverse cultures and foods. While in these countries, Ziva often volunteers her photographic services to non-profit organizations.

Originally from England, ANDY SHEEN-TURNER's (Food Stylist) career path has led him from restaurant chef to caterer to private chef and now to food stylist and culinary producer. His work has been seen on the Food Network, the Fine Living Network, in magazines, cookbooks, and on national television commercials. He currently lives in Los Angeles with his wife Lily.

LESLIE FEIBLEMAN (Marketing Director), a Los Angeles area native, is a senior film programmer and the director of special programs and outreach at the Newport Beach Film Festival, where she programs documentaries and narrative films, organizes filmmaking seminars and a youth and family film series. Leslie also works as the film curator for the Orange County Museum of Art where she hosts the *Cinema Orange* film series. She has a passion for bringing cultural programs to her community and connecting nonprofit organizations with the arts and entertainment worlds. A graduate of UC Berkeley with degree in Architecture, she enjoys cooking from her garden and currently lives with her husband and two children in Newport Beach, California.

After starting his Los Angeles career as a CNN correspondent, BRYCE ZABEL (Creative Consultant) turned to Hollywood where he has created five network television series and received writing credit on two major motion pictures. He recently served as Chairman and CEO of the Academy of Television Arts and Sciences, overseeing three Emmy awards shows and negotiating a record-breaking network license fee. In the last two years, Bryce has written three produced TV miniseries including *The Poseidon Adventure* and *Blackbeard*. He is a member of both the WGA and DGA as well as an adjunct professor at the USC School of Cinema and Television. However, what he considers his greatest productions are The Hollywood Cookbook website and his three children with his wife, Jackie.

Originally from Las Vegas, Nevada, DON MOSS (Legal Counsel) has been involved in the entertainment industry as an attorney, producer, and actor. He practices entertainment law with the Los Angeles firm of Troy & Gould, and, this year, celebrates his 30th wedding anniversary with his wife Alexa and children Alec and Caitlin.

Photo Credits

Food photographs courtesy of Craig T. Mathew, Ziva Santop, and Stock Food Agency

Jamie Gwen courtesy of Jamie Gwen

Thora Birch by Matt Baron/BEI Images

Michael Chiklis by Robert Zuckerman

Mario Batali headshot by Beatriz da Costa, food shot by Christopher Hirscheimer

Eric Close by Troy Meeder

Mark Dacascos by Kauila Barber

James Denton by Andrew Eccles/American Broadcasting Companies, Inc.

Michael Cimarusti by Steve Nilsson Photography

MJ Fox & Tracy Pollan by Getty Images/Matt Szwajkos

Brendan & Afton Fraser by John Solano, Sean Bolger

Rocco Dispirito by Henry Leutwyler

Greg Grunberg by Sheryl Nields/American Broadcasting Companies, Inc.

Anne Hathaway by Chris Militscher/Contour Photos

Paige Hemmis by Karen Bystedt

Ron Howard by Ron Batzdorff

Jane Kaczmarek and Bradley Whitford by Jean-Paul Assenard/WireImage

Esai Morales by Giulliano Bekor

Wolfgang Puck by Alex Berliner/Berliner Photography

Don Most by Dana Patrick

Bob Saget courtesy of Bob Saget

Joachim Splichal headshot and food shot courtesy of Patina Group

Marlo Thomas by Patrick Demarchelier

Kerry Washington by Paul Smith

Nick Stellino headshot by Nancy Stellino, food shot by Nick Stellino

Treat Williams courtesy of Treat Williams

Alicia Witt courtesy of Alicia Witt

Scott and Kelley Wolf by Vance Green

SILVERBACK
BOOKS INC.